"*Out of the Dust* is like Avis herself: challenging, inspiring, and real. Her story shows how God's power transcends background, abilities, and qualifications to make the ordinary extraordinary. Read it and watch God inspire you to move out the dust of your own background and into His perfect will."

Steve Long
Senior Leader, Catch the Fire Toronto

"Avis Goodhart's incredible journey is a wonderful breath of fresh Holy Spirit wind challenging our comfortable Western generation to say yes with all our hearts and bodies to the call of Jesus. Her laid-down life, willing to go to the poor and broken with only faith and courage, is a model of true discipleship. John Wimber once said spiritual consecration is saying to the Lord, 'I'm loose change in your pocket; spend me any way you want.' Avis walks in that experiential reality. This model of a "trickle-up revival" is the New Testament pattern of Jesus and Paul. Read and be challenged, convicted, and inspired to follow the same Lord that Avis does in running into the dark, not away from it."

Dan Slade
International Coordinator, Partners in Harvest, Toronto, Canada

"Everyone needs a personal hero of the faith. I am not talking about the Apostle Paul or King David but a modern-day hero who has walked out the faith under the most difficult of circumstances. The story of Avis Goodhart will encourage, stretch and inspire your faith as you follow her journeys in *Out of the Dust*. What do you do when God gives you a vision and you watch it die in front of you? Where does faith comes from when all seems lost? This is why I recommend you read and share this book. We all need a current story of someone who with God's help has turned tragedy into triumph."

Walker Moore
President and Founder, Awe Star Ministries, Tulsa, Oklahoma

"I met Avis at Casa de Paz when I brought mission teams to Pacasmayo, Peru to serve the Lord. I observed her passion in action as she told me her story and cared for the orphans of that region. It is clear that the Lord has ministered to the depths of her heart. She has allowed Him to use her time of brokenness to produce a unique understanding and love for those who are in need. The word "can't" is not part of her vocabulary. She does whatever it takes and inspires others to do likewise. *Out of the Dust: Story of an Unlikely Missionary* will inspire readers to overcome, regardless of the odds. Avis gets it. Avis lives it. Avis is the hands and feet of Jesus to those others have forgotten or ignored. Reading about her life, her story, and her journey is worth your time. Her testimony will produce new areas of surrender in yours!"

Brent Higgins
Associate Pastor, Parkview Baptist Church, Tulsa, Oklahoma;
Coauthor, *I Would Die for You*

"The various stories in Avis's life bring to life the redemptive power of the gospel of Jesus Christ. Her message is powerful and so humble. God blesses and esteems the contrite and the humble heart."

Maggie Baratto
Father's Heart Ministries;
Canadian Director for the International Association of Healing Rooms

"Having had the honor to know Avis for many years and to observe her love for God and for the Peruvian people, it's hard to imagine viewing her life as anything other than completely sold out to Jesus. *Out of the Dust* takes you down that life path and allows you to witness God's power of transformation whereby He takes an ordinary, broken person and moves His Holy Spirit over a life with amazing results."

Jim Johnson
President, JACA Holdings, and Tethco Technologies, Inc.

"I have read about Abraham and many others in the Bible who faithfully responded to God's calling to foreign lands without knowing all the trials (and blessings) that would follow. I have also been blessed with knowing present-day people like Avis Goodhart who are examples to us all that God hasn't changed. He is always faithful as we respond, in faith, to His calling. For those who are persuaded that God's story is fully contained in the books between Genesis and Revelation and that He somehow stopped functioning in biblical ways after those books were written, the life of Avis and many like her illustrate the truth: we serve a God who calls people to divine mission. He empowers and sustains them in the face of the obstacles they are sure to find as they work to advance His kingdom. Be inspired, and then seek the Lord for His calling on your life. You will be amazed, as Avis was, at how He manifests Himself in the process."

Reverend Jim King
Chaplain (retired)

"From nothing our Creator made everything. But from dust came the Creator's most glorious creation. Destiny is in the dust. Avis Goodhart's story *Out of the Dust* is living proof of this profound truth. Read it, and let her take you for a joy ride of quirky connections of kingdom significance. Discover, as Avis has, how God's presence can transform the pain, rejection, and sadness of life in ways that bring healing for body, soul, and spirit. With this revelation, Avis models the power and love of God in ways that bring the kingdom of heaven to earth. The good news is that we are all "unlikely" missionaries. And I know God will use Avis's story to encourage you in your own walk from dust to glory. Enjoy!"

Pastor Jeff McCracken
Pastor, Selah Fire Church, Drayton, Ontario, www.selahfire.com

"What a story! We got to read the book as it was being written. We met Avis in the 1970s and became lifelong friends. We have watched her spiritual growth over the years and how God has directed her life. We have also watched her obedience to His call. No matter the price or the sacrifice, she willingly answered. Many have been blessed by her love of the Lord. Thank you, Avis, for your example."

Herbert and Rachel Cypret
Board members, Go Ye Ministries

Out of the Dust

Watch Avis Goodhart's interview on *100 Huntley Street*

Out of the Dust

Story of an Unlikely Missionary

Avis Goodhart
With Marti Pieper

ANEKO Press

Vignette Artist: Elena Kalistratova/Shutterstock

Cover Design: Amber Burger

Editor: Ruth Zetek

Printed in the United States of America

www.lifesentencepublishing.com

LIFE SENTENCE Publishing books are available at discounted prices for ministries and other outreach. Find out more by contacting us at info@lspbooks.com

ANEKO Press, LIFE SENTENCE Publishing, and its logo are trademarks of LIFE SENTENCE Publishing, LLC

P.O. Box 652

Abbotsford, WI 54405

BIOGRAPHY & AUTOBIOGRAPHY / Religious

Paperback ISBN: 978-1-62245-223-1

Ebook ISBN: 978-1-62245-227-9

10 9 8 7 6 5 4 3 2 1

This book is available from www.amazon.com, Barnes & Noble, and your local bookstore.

Share this book on Facebook:

Details in some anecdotes and stories have been changed to protect the identities of the persons involved.

And if you spend yourselves in behalf of the hungry
and satisfy the needs of the oppressed,
then your light will rise in the darkness,
and your night will become like the noonday.

The LORD will guide you always;
he will satisfy your needs in a sun-scorched land
and will strengthen your frame.
You will be like a well-watered garden,
like a spring whose waters never fail.

Isaiah 58:10-11

I believe that before we are born, God places within us a particular personality with certain qualities, talents, and traits. He also picks our parents and siblings. I am so grateful to be in the family He chose.

This book is dedicated to my sisters and brothers, Rada, Bob, Art (deceased), Fred, George, and Carol; and to my kids by birth, Tia and Mark; and by marriage, Glen (deceased), Cindy, and Cleta.

It is also dedicated in memory of my parents, Bob and Elsie Miller. As Dad once said, "All these happy people because I loved Elsie and she loved me."

Avis Goodhart
Pacasmayo, Peru

Contents

Foreword

"I will write down all these things as a testimony of what the Lord will do" (Isaiah 8:16a NLT).

It's been said the only story God can't use is the one that isn't told. For twenty-six years, it has been my joy and privilege to help people tell their stories of His faithfulness on national Christian television. After her first appearance on *100 Huntley Street*, I knew Avis Goodhart's journey had to be detailed in a book.

Here is a woman who could have been defeated by past failures and harsh realities, but instead has showcased the truth of 1 Corinthians 1:27: God's strength shows up best in weak people. Avis leaves no room for doubting God has a plan and the power to bring it to fruition. As she said on our program, "God can use anybody to do anything. We just need to be willing to follow where He leads. God will use the things of our past – hurts, homelessness, abuse, as well as a good family life, education, and money. They all can be tools that God will use if we give them to Him. God was calling me: 'Go. I will show you what to do when you get there.'"

When the effects of Bell's palsy cost Avis her teaching job, she retired with two thirds of her salary until age sixty-five, providing the start-up funds for Go Ye Ministries. God's launch pad freed Avis to become ordained, incorporated, and prepared for Pacasmayo, Peru, and the church, orphanage, and school she founded.

In a place of loss and discouragement, God reignited a call to missions that Avis first sensed at age twelve. This testimony reminds us all that it is never too late to make a fresh start and perhaps discover our destiny and purpose.

"He lifts the poor from the dust and the needy from the garbage dump" (Psalm 113:7).

Moira Brown
100 Huntley Street
Toronto, Canada

Acknowledgments

God must have wanted this story written, or it would never have happened. Like so many things He has led me to do, I was and am incapable of doing the job. But through Him, we can do all things.

Each time I had the pleasure of appearing on *100 Huntley Street*, Moira Brown, host of *Crossroads*, would tell me, "You need to write a book." Two couples, Jim and Cathy Johnson and Tony and Mary Ann Geisen, heard Moira because they had driven me to the station and were watching the live program.

That's all the encouragement Jim needed. He started looking for a writer. In fact, the next week, he called the program and asked if they knew who could help. That eventually led us to Marti Pieper, who is now a good friend and collaborative writer of *Out of the Dust*.

Tony and Mary Ann live half the year in Canada and half the year in Peru. Every Sunday afternoon, they host all the volunteers from the Casa de Paz orphanage for a wonderful lunch and fellowship. After they heard what Moira said about writing a book, they came up with a plan. Every Sunday after lunch, they would stick a small tape recorder in front of me and ask a few questions. Mary Ann transcribed everything from these sessions.

Later, Bettina Neubauer, another volunteer from Canada,

spent several days with me as we put everything Mary Ann had written in order and added more to it. By the time Marti came to Peru, we had 130 pages of notes to share. Marti and I became fast friends as we worked on more. Marti followed me around for the next two weeks, doing what I did and interviewing everyone along the way. Marti returned home, and the work and phone calls began. It was really happening. Praise God!

I also want to thank all the people who accompanied me on those early mission trips to the mountains of Honduras, the jungles of Colombia, and down the Amazon, and over the mountains of Peru. God bless you, Daniel Ortega, Helen Blair, Steve Claypool, Fred and Peggy Miller, George and Mary Miller, and so many more. God blessed us as we ministered to others. Also, many thanks to Lorene Vickery who keeps Go Ye Ministries' books straight and packed so many shoeboxes, blessing thousands of children through the years.

God blessed Go Ye Ministries and me very much through Rachel and Herb Cypert, Al and Charlotte Lockhart, Helen Blair, Jim and Cathy Johnson, Pastor Jeff McCracken, Mike and Jan Bayton, Mary Ann and Tony Giesen, Roseana Giegler, Emma Mier, Arada and George Steinann, George and Mary Miller, Fred and Peggy Miller, Mike and Mary Ann Traylor, Roger Bill and Ruth Remington, Kevin Guier, Bruce Goulding, Mandy Kauer, Tammy Dicken, Jana and Wayne Salley, and the list goes on. God knows, and He will bless.

Thank you also to the many children and families God has allowed me to serve through the years. You have my heart and my prayers always.

Avis Goodhart
Pacasmayo, Peru

CHAPTER 1

Preparing the Way

‿✦‿

*P*recious things often carry a high price tag. That explains why most of the big decisions in my life have begun with a spiritual battle. My journey into missions did too.

You could say I'm a late bloomer. I married at eighteen and had my first child before my nineteenth birthday, but other things took me longer. I didn't graduate from college until my mid-forties. I didn't start my career teaching special education until after that. And, at age fifty, I'd never gone out of the United States on a mission trip.

In 1995, that final fact changed. And so did my life.

My missionary calling began in childhood, and once I started teaching, it grew stronger and stronger. I spent every school year praying about missions and asking God how He wanted me to use my summer vacation. For two summers in a row, my teenage nieces and I took our own mission trips. We painted the words to John 3:16 across matching T-shirts and wore them as we drove across the United States, stopping at campgrounds all along the way.

I taught the girls how to have conversations that helped move people toward faith. "Do you know about Jesus?" we asked everyone we met. I was proud of my traveling team, but our work didn't seem like enough. I wanted to do more. I wanted to go farther.

I wanted to be a missionary.

By the 1994-95 school year, my desire to serve overseas had grown to the point that, by faith, I bought my passport. Next, I wrote letters to several large mission organizations to let them know of my availability and willingness to pay my way. Simple, right?

Wrong. Not one of the organizations wrote me back. What did God have in mind?

My longing for missions became a heavy weight pressing in on my spirit. If I saw a child on a street corner, I visualized him crying out for help. If I heard the word *nations* in the music we sang at church, my tears flowed – and I'm not a person who likes to cry. I couldn't seem to think about anything but missions. But I had nowhere to go, and no way to get there.

One day that fall, I decided to have it out with the Lord. We met, as usual, in my big blue chair. "God," I told Him. "I can't cry for the rest of my life. Either take this desire away or show me what to do."

He brought to mind a church I'd visited more than once in Grove, Oklahoma. I'd heard the pastor's wife there speak about mission trips. I'm sure she didn't remember me (we met at a convention among more than five hundred women), but that wouldn't stop me. Not now.

I went straight to the phone, looked up her number, and called. When a woman answered, I knew this was it. I'd reached someone who could help me at last.

"You don't know me, but I remember you. I'm Avis Goodhart, and I've got to get to the mission field. Can you help?"

My words stumbled over themselves as I continued. "I'm a teacher, so I can go in the summertime." In case that didn't sound enthusiastic enough, I added, "I'll do anything – dig ditches, whatever. I just want to go."

I wanted to let her know about the money too. "I can pay for myself. Just please, please help me connect with a mission trip or a missionary. Something, somebody," I said. "I have to go, and I have to go soon."

Laughter floated from the other end of the phone line. *Surely a pastor's wife wouldn't laugh at my desire for missionary service. Or would she?* My spirit dropped to my shoes.

Precious things often carry a high price tag.

I finally paused long enough to let her respond. "I'm not the pastor's wife. But guess what? I'm a missionary home on leave. My name's Karen."

For the rest of that school year, Karen, her husband Dale, and I talked every few weeks. I would drive over to Grove to meet with them and before long, we all knew it: God was calling me to serve in Honduras, where they served full-time for six years. They told me about Pastor Roberto Ventura and the church he founded in the capital city, Tegucigalpa (Tegus for short). Gerizim Church had grown to a membership of more than three thousand people. Surely God could find a place for me there.

We made the arrangements. After school let out, I'd fly to Tegus and serve under Pastor Ventura. I was nervous, but excited. I could respond to God's call at last. I knew I'd miss my husband, but I could hardly wait to go.

But I wanted to bring more than myself to Honduras. Karen and Dale told me about the terrible poverty there and made arrangements for me to work with the only two English-speaking women in Gerizim Church. They would translate for me while I served both the church and an orphanage outside Tegus.

I was going to an orphanage, and I knew I couldn't go without supplies. I started collecting clothes and anything else

I thought the orphans might need from my friends, church, students, and whoever was willing to give. I shipped several hundred pounds of goods and, as my departure day drew near, had six hundred more pounds to take with me.

I called the airport a few days before I left to make sure the tubs of supplies would fit on my flight. "Sure," they told me. "Bring 'em along. We'll get everything on somehow."

Excited about my opportunity, my daughter Tia drove up from her Florida home to help me pack. And pack we did. Bin after bin of T-shirts, jeans, videos, and other gifts for the orphans filled my living room. When Tia drove me to the Tulsa airport, we took along her two preteen children, her baby in a stroller, and of course, the huge Rubbermaid bins full of supplies.

"I'm sorry," the man at the ticket counter said when we attempted to check our unusual baggage. "You can't travel with all these. You'll have to choose what to leave behind."

"But I called ahead," I pushed back. "These are supplies for orphans in Honduras. What will the children do without them?"

For all the good my questions did, I might as well have said the supplies were for aliens in outer space. So Tia and I did the only thing we knew: we prayed. Together, we gripped the stroller handle and marched back and forth near the ticket counter. The baby's screams added to the overall chaos.

"I'm not going without the tubs, you know," I spoke out when the man from the airlines approached again. "I'll pay extra. I don't care – I want them down there, so get them on the plane." Our little team kept marching and praying, our only accompaniment the baby's now-occasional sobs.

Suddenly, a different airline employee in a dark uniform appeared. "Ma'am?" he said hesitantly.

"Yes, sir?"

"We've got the room. My supervisor says the tubs can go."

Hallelujah! I knew my God could turn a mess into a message.

I was so excited I was shaking as I hugged my family good-bye and boarded the plane. After all the waiting, all the praying, all the obstacles and dead ends, I was on my way at last.

As we landed in Honduras, joy overwhelmed me. I'd reached the mission field! I stumbled through Customs and Immigration, unsure of what to do next. I had confidence in God's calling, but I'd never left the country before.

"Don't forsake me now, Lord," I kept repeating as uniformed strangers asked questions in a language I didn't speak. Who was this crazy American, and what did she have in all those plastic tubs? I kept a smile on my face and attempted to explain.

At last, all my luggage and I made it through the final checkpoint and into the main part of the airport. Conversations swirled around me, but I didn't understand a word. Smells assaulted my nose, but I recognized none. Hundreds of people moved around me, but nobody looked familiar.

You can imagine my delight when I saw a slight, dark-haired woman holding up a homemade placard that bore my name in slanting letters: "AVIS GOODHART." This was Gladys Montoya, one of the translators from Gerizim Church. "Welcome to Honduras!" she smiled as she asked for a porter's help in moving the tubs to her waiting vehicle.

Gladys loved Jesus, and it showed. She drove straight to her home and, in spite of the late hour, brought me a heaping plate of food. It smelled heavenly and tasted even better.

While I was eating, Gladys slipped out and came back with a basin of warm water. She knelt and removed my shoes.

"What are you doing?" I asked in amazement.

"Please, I want to wash your feet," Gladys looked up, tears in her eyes. "You came to my country because you love my Jesus. You must let me do this."

Allowing Gladys to bathe my feet as she bowed before me was the most humbling moment of my life. That day, we began a friendship that lasted through many mission trips, many service projects, and many souls won for the kingdom. And God would use all these experiences to reshape the direction of my life.

I just didn't know it at the time.

Out of the Dust:
Earlene Matthews

I'm not the only one who had to wait to fulfill her calling. One of the first people to accompany me on a mission trip was a precious sister in Christ named Earlene Matthews. As a young woman, she had five years of missionary training only to have her sponsoring organization decide not to send her to the field because she had no husband. Although she worked in their home office until she retired, the great regret of her life was never having served overseas.

At the time I met Earlene, her eyes were weak and painful, but her spirit was strong and alive. She loved hearing stories about my mission trips. And after I learned her background, I knew God wanted me to take her along.

Earlene, now legally blind, came with me on a medical mission trip to Honduras in 1997. I had to lead her off the plane onto the tarmac, but she had no fear. She would go anyplace and do anything to share the gospel.

Our team spent three days on that trip holding a clinic high in the mountains. Early in the morning, people lined up to see the doctor, then came through our evangelistic line before receiving their medicine. Three or four volunteer teams waited, each with its own translator, ready to share the gospel. That's where my friend found her ministry.

It didn't take long before everyone knew God was doing something special on the bench where Earlene and her translator (a team all by themselves) were seated. As people came through her line, Earlene would ask her translator to give them a Bible and open it to a specific place. When she was sure her audience was ready, she recited the passage by heart and explained its meaning. Next, she led her listeners to passage after passage, quoting each one from memory.

Earlene would then ask, "Isn't God good?" or "Would you like to talk to Him? He's waiting."

She sat on her bench all day, sharing the message of God's love not only to the people in her line, but to the doctor and other clinic workers. In those three days, she alone led more than one hundred people to Christ. She was overwhelmed with gratitude and joy as she watched her dream become reality.

After we returned to Tegus, Earlene had the opportunity to speak in a home group for young people. She sat, unnoticed, in the patio area as the teens arrived, laughing and talking among themselves until the host introduced her.

With the same technique she used at the clinic, Earlene began to teach. Asking the students to open their Bibles to a particular passage, she quoted it from memory and explained its meaning. She recited verse after verse, threading them together in her lesson. At one point, she paused, and the room of about forty young adults fell silent.

"When I was a young girl," she told her listeners, "God put a desire in my heart to memorize His Word. I'm so grateful I did, because today, no one and nothing – not even blindness – can take it away from me." She paused again as she finished. "I have it right here in my heart."

I could see what Earlene couldn't: unshed tears glistening in eyes throughout the room. That night, many of the young people committed to hide God's Word in their hearts. And many asked Him to make them more like Earlene.

I thank the Lord for bringing the two of us together and for giving her the opportunity – at last – to take her gifts and her ministry to the ends of the earth.

CHAPTER 2

Growing Up Different

L ong before my missionary adventures began, I realized I didn't do things the same way others did. My drive to be different must have begun during my childhood.

Our family's life *was* different from that of most families during the mid-1940s and 1950s. After World War II ended, people seemed happy to discover a new normal. GI loans allowed soldiers to buy new houses, which sprang up everywhere. Jobs were plentiful. The future looked good. By the mid-1950s, most American homes sported televisions, countertop stoves, and refrigerators.

But something about our family (I'm the oldest of seven children) was different. It started with my father.

"He's got problems from the war," Mom explained. She repeated these words many times through the years, usually when she had to excuse one of Dad's crazy decisions or angry outbursts.

Today, we call his condition PTSD (Post-Traumatic Stress Disorder). Back then, no one recognized it. No one even discussed it.

One way Dad dealt with his problems was to come home

and, with no prior warning, pack up and move our family to another location. We moved and moved, sometimes as often as every few days or months.

In one year of upheaval, we kids went to ten different schools. One day, we would have a nice house. The next, Dad would come home with a crazy story like: "They're watching me. They got people spying on me all the time. We gotta get outta here. Now."

Dad dropped out of school in the eighth grade to help support his family. Once he turned eighteen, he served in the army. After the war ended, he passed a test that would have allowed him to attend Ohio's Kent State University even without a high school diploma. But once again, his PTSD got in the way. Dad never went to one college class.

While in Kent, my parents rented a little house, and Dad got a job in a machine shop. The owner, a strong Christian, began teaching him the tool- and die-making trade.

Before long, this same man invited my parents to attend church services, where they both accepted Christ. After that, as Mom put it, "All hell broke loose." And there began Dad's lifetime succession of jobs and moves.

But that didn't mean he was stupid. Not a bit. Whenever I had a difficult math problem, I asked for his help. He could do almost any calculation in his head. "It's an easy answer, honey," he would say as he sat down beside me.

"But Dad, I need more than just the answer. I have to show my teacher how I got it," I would explain. "Can you show me how to do it so I can understand it myself?"

Dad could tell me the answer but couldn't explain how he got it. "I don't know; just fill in something," he said with a shrug. I knew not to ask more questions.

Dad's mind flipped back and forth from reality to confusion. He would have a good job and talk about it with confidence, even boasting. Then his more negative mindset crept in. "I know they're going to fire me" or "They're watching everything I do." Convinced of his employers' evil intentions, he would quit before they let him go.

When Dad came home with moving orders, we all knew what to do: sweep our few clothes and supplies into whatever boxes and bags we could find, stuff anything we could in the trunk, tie everything else on the roof, and head straight for nowhere – fast. Often, we slipped out of town before dawn. We slept in the car, on picnic tables, alongside the road, behind billboards, or in Salvation Army shelters when we found one.

We all got used to this odd routine. But in July 1953, something worse happened. I was almost nine; Arada (Rada), seven; Bobby, six; Art, four; Freddy, three; George, eighteen months; and our youngest sister, Carol, was only two weeks old. For the past few months, most of our family had stayed with an uncle and his family. But one morning, his wife decided she'd had enough. She drove all nine of us – Mom, Dad, and seven children – to a neighboring county, put us out alongside the road, and drove away. *Where could we go?*

Somehow we made it to a nearby park with the belongings we'd stuffed into a few suitcases and a box or two. But we still needed a place to spend the night. Mom and Dad went to scout out some sleeping arrangements. They placed newborn Carol on a bed pillow on the ground, giving my next-younger sister and me orders for their absence.

"Don't leave the park," Mom cautioned. "And whatever you do, don't take the baby off the pillow."

Even at seven and eight, Rada and I understood obedience. When we wanted to move from the slide to the swings, we each picked up two corners of the pillow so we could move baby and pillow together. After a few rounds of this and an hour or more in the park, little Carol started to cry. She cried, and cried, and kept on crying.

Rada and I looked at each other in desperation. *What should we do now?* Rada had watched Mom fix the baby's bottles (I stayed with another relative until a few days before our sudden eviction), so she opened a bottle and dumped in some Karo syrup and canned milk. "Now, we gotta add water," Rada instructed. "Let's go over to the drinking fountain." We struggled to hoist pillow and baby once more.

Because of our small size, neither of us could do the job alone. My sister climbed up and held the bottle under the spigot while I turned the handle.

"We gotta shake it up good," she said. "That's real important."

Preparation accomplished, Rada stuck the rubber nipple into still-screaming Carol's mouth. The crying stopped. Once again, life was good, but our peace didn't last.

We noticed a lady watching from a white frame house down the street. Every so often, she came out on her front porch and waved. We stopped what we were doing whenever we saw her, but once she went back inside, we returned to our games.

We soon realized she was on her way over. We also realized she intended to question us. Always the protective oldest sister, I hopped off the slide and stood beside baby Carol, now fast asleep. Rada, as usual, followed right behind me.

"What a beautiful little doll baby," the woman cooed. "Hey, it's alive!"

"Yes, she's my sister," I spoke up. Our visitor bent over. *How can I stop her?*

"You can't pick her up off the pillow! Mama said!"

She stepped back. This time, she tried a new tactic. "Where are your mommy and daddy?"

"They're coming right back," I said firmly. "We're just waiting."

"But you've been here a long time. Aren't you hungry?"

With that, she struck a chord. Our morning drive-and-drop hadn't included breakfast, but I knew better than to beg.

"Mommy and Daddy are coming right back, and they'll get us some food. We're just playing."

Carol picked that moment to resume her cries. By this time, she had soaked her diaper too. The kind woman tried once more. "I live right there [pointing down the block]. I could take you over and give you all a sandwich."

I remained firm. "Mommy said to stay in the park."

"You wouldn't have to go inside." Her voice warmed. "I've got a table and benches behind the house. And chocolate milk."

I wonder what it's like to have a real house, a clean bed, and go to only one school.

By this time, the other kids were listening. And if the offer of sandwiches didn't win them over, the chocolate milk did.

"You can't pick up the baby," I cautioned. Again, Rada and I moved to opposite sides of the pillow, and our little band started off. Now that we had to move Carol more than a few feet, we struggled.

By this time, our benefactor was wise to our ways. "Let me help. I won't pick up the baby; I'll just carry the pillow." I allowed this but still clung to one corner.

The luncheon excursion seemed like a visit to paradise. Our new friend brought out a tray loaded with sandwiches, sliced apples, and the promised chocolate milk. "My husband's a doctor," she said. "He works long hours, so I'm glad to have the company."

I looked around the yard. Flowers bloomed in several beds, and a painted windmill stood in one corner. I thought what I always thought when we passed comfortable homes: *I could live in a house like this.* When I saw a little girl about my size playing in front of what seemed like a nice house, my thoughts stretched further: *I wonder what it's like to have a real house, a clean bed, and go to only one school.*

Our happy lunch almost finished, we looked up to see our

parents standing over us. The nice lady had watched them return to the park and waved them over. "You have the sweetest children," she said. "I invited them for lunch."

"Thank you, ma'am," Dad spoke up. "You're very kind, but we've got it under control. Kids, time to go now."

Obediently, we followed our parents across town to the VFW (Veterans of Foreign Wars) hall, where an administrator promised us beds for the night. "Avis, you shouldn't have left the park," Mom told me later. "Still, it was good that she fed you."

I stayed quiet, thankful Mom and Dad didn't make a big deal out of our adventure and for a kind woman with a tray full of sandwiches and chocolate milk. But I couldn't help but wonder what would happen next.

Out of the Dust:
Elisabeth

I understand an oldest girl who takes responsibility for her siblings – especially when her family lives in constant crisis. That explains my special connection with Elisabeth.

One day, her mother came to talk to us at our orphanage, Casa de Paz. "I'll leave my kids with you during the week and keep them myself on the weekends," she said. We knew this wouldn't work. For a while, we gave her some money so she could afford to stay home with her children.

After months of indecision, Elisabeth's mom was ready. She wanted her children – Elisabeth and three younger brothers – to live in the orphanage. The social worker was visiting Casa de Paz that day, so I drove her and Pastor Jeff McCracken from Canada, serving with us that week, out to their home.

"Rough" would be a kind word to describe it. With stucco walls and a dirt floor, it looked like many of those that surround

us here in Peru. One of the first things we noticed was a pig tied up behind the tiny house. To prevent the neighbors from stealing him, the family brought him inside at night and chained him to their bed. Not exactly a pig in a blanket, but close enough to make me shudder.

"I want to stay and work in the fields with Mama," Elisabeth told us as her tears overflowed. "The more money we make, the sooner we can bring the boys home."

I took a deep breath. "Honey, if you do that, you may help your mom right now, but you won't be able to do much." I knew how to speak her language. "And you won't have anyone to take care of the boys."

She looked at me, unconvinced. I added, "If you come with us and get an education, you can become a secretary, a teacher, whatever you want." I reached back into my memories to touch her heart. "If you work the fields, in ten years, fifteen years, you'll still be working the fields. But if you get an education, in ten years, you and your family will have a whole new life."

I couldn't tell whether Elisabeth heard me or not. Her face remained stoic, and she didn't respond. But her mother was listening. And before long, she had talked her oldest daughter into coming to the orphanage with the other children.

Last spring, Elisabeth finished high school. She works in a nearby store and continues her education outside the orphanage. Little by little, she's saving money and fixing up the family home. She knows that someday the combination of faith and hard work will bring her family home at last.

CHAPTER 3

On the Road Again

Although I hoped we'd visit our sandwich-making friend again, we only stayed one night in that small town. In fact, our family never stayed long in any one place before we were on the road again.

Dad was determined to make it out to the West Coast. He'd contracted a lung infection and was sure a dry climate would improve his health. He coerced Mom once again into calling her father for money. The man we called Pop was upstanding, hard-working, and never failed to express his disappointment in our lifestyle. Still, he always sent the funds.

Dad's PTSD left him mixed up about many things. But on the road, he had a plan, and he knew how to work it. He liked to hit the county seats ("They're sure to have a place we can stay"). At the local VFW, he'd explain to the person in charge, "I'm a veteran with an honorable medical discharge, but I could use some help."

At that point, he'd look around at the seven of us kids as if to emphasize the need. "You see, we're on our way to California where I've got a real good job lined up." Another pause. "But we had to spend all our cash to [fix our car, pay the hospital bill, or whatever story Dad came up with at the time]. We could sure use some gas money. And is there a way you could put us up for the night?"

We waited, hopeful, as the supervisor considered this long request. I don't know if it was his veteran status, his sad story, or the real presence of a wife and seven young children, but Dad almost always got what he wanted.

If that didn't work, or if the town didn't have a VFW, he'd hit up the Red Cross or Salvation Army. I liked the Salvation Army best. Sometimes they gave us clothes, which we always needed.

Dad made sure not to visit the same county seat twice. His sales pitches netted us lots of free meals and any number of nights lined up on cots at the VFW hall or crammed into a cheap motel room. But sometimes, necessity became the mother of invention.

Once, when I was about ten or eleven, we were cooped up in the car because of the winter weather. Dad kept it running day and night so we could stay warm, stopping once in a while to scrounge up a few dollars for gas.

Mom and Dad, seven children, and our assorted belongings filled our big old Hudson. The windows fogged from the combination of our hot breath inside and the ice-cold air outside. Lying on the shelf behind the back seat, I stared into the night at the stars hanging over the frozen countryside. But I also noticed Dad rubbing his eyes.

At this point, we'd been driving for days with only quick rest stops. On these cross-country adventures, Mom never drove. She was too busy playing navigator for Dad, who could get lost going around the block.

"I can't do it anymore," he said as we neared a roadside park. "I've got to stretch out."

Dad stopped beside a cement picnic table. He got out of the car, brushed the snow from the table, and took our big bag of dirty clothes out of the trunk. We watched from the car, silent, as he scattered them over the tabletop.

"Come on, Avis, Rada, Bob. We'll sleep out here." He must have noticed our stunned expressions because he added, "If we stay close together, we'll keep warm. And Mom and the little kids will have room to stretch out. Let's go."

As we three oldest children untangled ourselves and stumbled out of the car, Dad brought a couple of blankets from the trunk. We snuggled close as he lay down beside us and pulled our covers on top.

Just because you don't have money doesn't mean you're broke.

Soon, we all drifted off. Just as Dad said, our combined body heat kept us from freezing. And right after sunrise, we were off the table and back on the road again.

Another memory reminds me of Dad's resourcefulness – and my determination to follow a different path. We ran out of gas one hot afternoon on Route 66. About half a mile down the highway stretching through the desert stood a single ranch house.

"They'll give gas to kids easier than to a grownup," Dad told Rada and me. "Go ask for a couple gallons."

He knew most ranchers kept a big gas tank to fill up their vehicles. "Just ask. It won't hurt them to share."

My sister and I knew better than to refuse. Dad would just keep talking until we finally complied.

With hearts much heavier than the rusty gas can we carried, we trudged toward the ranch. I didn't want to ask for gas. *Just because you don't have money doesn't mean you're broke*, I thought. Even back then, I trusted God as my provider. *There's got to be a better way.*

The two of us walked down the road and turned, crossing some battered railroad tracks onto the long, dusty driveway. Once again, Dad's methods bore fruit. At the house, we stammered out our request, and the family filled our gas can. While an older boy handled the chore, Rada and I played with some puppies tumbling around in the dirt.

"Thank you," we chorused as we picked up the now-sloshing can and made our way back down the drive. But one of the puppies followed. "Go home!" we warned. Cute though he was, we knew better than to add an animal to our traveling road show.

Then the unbelievable happened. Rada and I hauled the can across the tracks, and the tiny dog ran to catch up. But just as an oncoming train blew its whistle, his paws got stuck. We rushed forward, then back as the engine bore down.

By now, we were screaming, shouting anything to get the puppy off the track. But it was too late. We watched in horror as the huge locomotive crushed him.

Two sobbing girls returned to the car, determined never to expect handouts. If we had our way, we'd never beg again.

Somewhere along the road, I got sick, so sick that Mom and Dad rented a couple of cabins: one for us kids and another for the two of them. I received extra-special treatment. "Don't disturb Avis," Mom told the others. But I was too sick to care.

Even the smell of food made me nauseous, but Mom kept coaxing me to eat. As a special treat, she put six-month-old Carol in with me. But the room, the baby – everything was spinning. All I could do was lift my head once in a while to make sure Carol was all right. We both survived my illness somehow.

After two weeks, I started feeling a little better. The rent was due, so we got ready to hit the road again. Mom took all four boys into a service station bathroom to scrub them up and dress them in clean clothes. "Just because we're poor doesn't mean we're dirty," Mom said for the millionth time.

Next, we girls had our turn. As I climbed out of the car, Mom turned her head to stare. "Avis! Even the whites of your eyes are yellow. You've got yellow jaundice!"

I'd never heard of yellow jaundice (hepatitis), so I didn't know how serious it could be. And even though I had improved by that time, Mom and Dad still felt sorry for me. They handed over the unheard-of sum of thirty-five cents to buy a candy bar for each child. I'm not sure what we did with the one for baby Carol, but I know it didn't go to waste.

Somehow, we made it out to California, where we again rented two cabins. After the long days and nights in the car, even lumpy beds and a sandy backyard felt like luxury.

But our rest didn't last long. Mom was washing clothes out back when she crumpled to the ground, unconscious. An ambulance came screaming up the road.

"Pneumonia and hepatitis," the doctor said. And after the staff investigated, they put me in the hospital too. I loved the firm bed and clean sheets but hated the poking and prodding. And the absolute bed rest was nothing any active child would welcome.

After some testing, the nurses told Mom, "Her heart and liver are scarred. Her organs may never grow any bigger, which will put a strain on her body as she grows."

Only nine years old, I already knew enough to be upset. The staff had transferred Mom and me to a county hospital because, as one haughty nurse in a starched white uniform said, "People like you don't belong here."

My face burned with shame as I carried on a silent argument. *I'm just a kid. I can't do anything about it. When I'm bigger, I'll get a job and work. And I'll never take anything from anyone again.*

My resolution didn't last long, but not because I didn't mean it. Right after the hospital released me, a television personality learned of our family's plight. Dad hauled us up to the studio, certain we'd hit the big time.

Not quite. The television people lined us up in birth order

for an appeal: "If anyone has a job for this deserving veteran, call us at KLAC-13. We'll put you in touch."

A huge car whisked us off after the interview to the mansion owned by one of the bigwig television producers. Realizing we were both the oddballs and the centerpiece of the evening, I didn't like the situation one bit.

"How old are you?" "Do you like living in a cabin?" "Since your mom is sick, do you handle the cooking?" The too-kind people in the too-fancy clothes spewed all these questions and more. Dad and the younger kids enjoyed the attention, but I recognized pity when I saw it.

Mom's right. It's better to work hard than ask for handouts. But I'm not old enough to help. How can I make them understand? In despair, I crept down the carpeted hallway. Locking the bathroom door, I buried my head in the plush towel hanging from the rack. *How can the world have so much and some people so little?*

By the time a kind lady found me, I was sitting on the floor, head in my hands. *They don't understand. We're no different from rich kids. On the inside, we're all the same.*

I hadn't noticed, but I'd torn the towel rack right off the wall.

Out of the Dust:
Juana Victoria

You can see how God gave me a heart for families who have to work hard just to survive. When I first met Juana, she was trying to mix mud in the dust, sand, and wind of Las Palmeras. A widow with five small children, she wanted to make adobe bricks so she could build a home. Juana's mother lived in the area, but her husband, a fisherman, had drowned in a storm at sea off the coast of Pacasmayo. He had been gone about eighteen months, and their youngest child was only about two years old.

No one would hire Juana, though, because she suffered from terrible epileptic seizures. Employers didn't want to risk her falling down in a seizure while cooking, cleaning, or climbing a ladder. But she is one of the hardest-working women I've ever met, and she would take whatever jobs she could get.

She learned to cut hair somehow and would go from house to house giving haircuts and pedicures. For a while, she worked in a clinic for some German people who gave her anti-seizure medication. But even that didn't stop the seizures completely, and because she loved her children and had to support them, she begged for work wherever she could find it.

I met Juana in 1997 when I was walking around the dump looking at the mess for the first time. Although her husband had been a Christian, Juana was not. But this day her heart was open and soft to the gospel. When we told her about Jesus, she believed.

Juana was healed of her epilepsy after we prayed over her during a church service. Only none of us realized it at the time. She didn't feel or act differently, and as far as we know, nothing spectacular happened. But one day not long after our time of prayer, she noticed she wasn't having seizures anymore. And she's never had a single one since.

Juana got connected with a university in Trujillo not long afterward, selling their brand-new correspondence courses. She received her payment in the form of courses she could take herself. This amazing woman earned a social work degree while continuing to raise her children and do all sorts of jobs. She eventually got a government job working with abused women and children, but that ended when the local government changed. She still does more than one job and even has a radio show where she brings in some of the government and other officials she became acquainted with through her work.

Juana brings her faith into everything she does. She is always encouraging to others, and no one can tell her God has no power because she's seen His healing work in her own life. She knows He will be just as faithful to bring others out of the dust.

CHAPTER 4

Unspeakable

Many of the orphans God brings us have suffered deep hurts. I can see it in the dullness of their eyes. And even when these little ones are smiling, they seem sad.

When they don't know I'm watching, I notice the pain in their eyes. They have a distant look, as though they're thinking about something too deep for words.

They don't cry or frown. But tension lingers on each face. I understand that tension, because I've suffered the unspeakable too.

I realize now how young I must have been when it began. Every time our travels took us near northeastern Ohio and Mom's relatives, we paid them a visit. Mom's father lived on the family farm with his daughters and son-in-law: Alice, who never married, and Ruth, Jim's vibrant, dark-haired wife. Mom's brother and his wife lived a few miles away.

I loved them all, especially Uncle Jim. I even called him "Daddy Jim." And that only added to my struggles. First of all, Pop's house was way out in the country. And Uncle Jim always seemed to find some excuse to bring me along on his errands: "Avis? Wanna come to the store with me to get some milk?"

Of course I wanted to go – at first. I don't remember much about those trips, but I do remember being young enough to stand up on the front seat of the car. But the comforting feel of the plushy seat cover couldn't make up for what happened there.

If I close my eyes, I can still see it: a man's hand in a rolled-up blue sleeve, reaching toward me. I shrink back against the seat, but I can't escape. I press up tight against the door.

Still, the hand finds me. And I don't know what to do.

Throughout my childhood, this scene repeated itself over and over. "Don't tell anyone," Uncle Jim would say, handing me a bright paper pinwheel or some other cheap toy. Only years later did I recognize these gifts for what they were.

But Uncle Jim didn't need to buy my silence. I was still the strong oldest girl who took care of everybody else. I didn't want to upset Pop or my aunts. I didn't tell anybody what happened in the car. In fact, I tried not to think about it.

Until the next time.

The most difficult episodes took place when I was eight years old. Mom and Dad left all of us kids with her family while they went to Wichita, Kansas, where Dad's family lived. Their plan was to get jobs and a place to live, then come and get us.

But life got in the way of their plans. They did get jobs and rented a cute little farmhouse just outside the city. But then Dad's mother was diagnosed with cancer, and he and Mom had to pitch in to help.

Rada and I stayed with Pop and his crew of adult children. Our brothers lived at Uncle Tag's, the next farm down the road.

On the surface, living at Pop's house seemed like a wonderful idea. Aunt Ruth stayed home to keep the house spotless and cook delicious meals. Rada and I loved everything she set before us: real dinners with meat, vegetables, and sometimes homemade brownies for dessert. We learned proper manners and felt like real ladies eating with the grownups. Instead of trying to wash up in gas station restrooms, we bathed in a tub filled with hot water. Instead of squeezing ourselves and our belongings into the car, we slept in a soft bed covered in warm quilts. And our aunts also let us have a bedtime snack every night – something we never heard of in our gypsy life with Mom and Dad.

Living here also meant something special for Rada, vision-impaired since birth. Aunt Alice took time to enroll her in a special school and made sure that, for the first time ever, she had glasses to improve her vision. Although Rada didn't enjoy the school (she could see better than most of the other students), we were both thankful to have such a loving aunt.

I know they'll come. They'll make everything all right.

Christmas this year looked different than ever before. We helped decorate the sparkling tree in the living room. Our aunts took us shopping, urging, "Don't peek" as they smuggled in all sorts of mysterious gifts.

They also began talking about us staying to live with them full-time.

"When we go to court, make sure to tell the judge you want to live here," Aunt Ruth urged. I didn't want to hurt her, but the terrible secret locked inside me refused to go away.

One night during dinner, Uncle Jim looked at me, and I knew. No one else saw, no one else noticed – but I did. I couldn't talk about it, didn't know what to call it or why it was wrong, but I knew.

Leaving my mashed potatoes and gravy to grow cold, I jumped up and ran out the door. Leaping over the ditch, I darted into the fields behind the barn. I ran, and ran, and ran, unaware that my frantic aunts and uncle were searching for me.

The whole time I ran, I kept watching for Mom and Dad to come driving down the road. *I know they'll come. They'll make everything all right.*

Instead, only Aunt Alice came after what seemed like hours. She found me lying in the weeds, exhausted and hopeless. "Avis! Why would you want to run away?" she puffed. "We're giving you and your sister such a good home. Come with me right now!"

When we got back to the house, all the adults seemed so upset. And they all had questions I couldn't answer. All except Uncle Jim. He stayed quiet while the others talked to me about "responsibility" and "gratitude" and other big words I didn't know.

I still couldn't answer their questions. I just felt sad all the time.

Running away didn't help anything. I often walked to the edge of the huge green yard, standing in the shade of the great old trees and looking down the dirt road. I was still hoping to see Mom and Dad coming to my rescue. No one knew what was wrong, and I couldn't share my awful secret. *Uncle Jim's a grown-up. This must be my fault. And I can't tell anyone. It would hurt Aunt Ruth too much.*

Despite my childish thinking, I knew what was happening was wrong. The problem had now gone far beyond inappropriate touching during car trips. Our grandfather was a night watchman. When he left for work, Rada and I slept in his bed. She slept next to the wall, and I took the outside.

What neither my sister nor anyone else knew was that, once Rada had fallen asleep, Uncle Jim would come to the bed, pick me up, and carry me into his bedroom. "Shhhhh," he'd whisper. "Be quiet! Don't wake anyone up." He always put me back next to Rada before Aunt Ruth came to bed.

The dirty, shameful feeling I felt after these nighttime visits lasted for years. And for years, I couldn't tell anyone what had happened. Who knew that one day I would care for orphans who had some of those same horrors in their past? And who knew that one day, sharing my story would bring other women freedom?

Only God. Only God, who brings beauty from ashes and hope from despair. And only God could bring me out of the dust of childhood abuse and into a life of serving other victims of the unspeakable.

Out of the Dust: Sophia

Sophia was one of those victims. When she and her two brothers came to us, she was a skinny, dirty eleven-year-old. She looked like most of the other orphan girls did at intake (our procedure for moving them into the orphanage), but with one important difference.

"Que está embarazada." The attending doctor hurried over to tell me.

I don't know many more Spanish words than I did when I first came to Peru, but I knew that one. "Pregnant? She can't be pregnant. She's eleven years old!"

As our staff spent more time with Sophia, her story came out in bits and pieces. Her mother – like many mothers in Peru – had a live-in boyfriend who was supporting the family. The home had only two beds, so the boys slept in one, and Sophia, her mother, and the boyfriend in the other.

You can guess what happened. Every night, the boyfriend took his choice of either Sophia or her mother. "Don't tell," her mother urged the little girl. "Without him, we have no food."

We don't know how long Sophia suffered the unspeakable. But one day, she got the courage to take her brothers and run. The three bedraggled children wound up at their grandmother's nearby home.

When the mother found them, she exploded. Grandma called the police, and not long after that, we got a call too. The judge had decided to place the children at Casa de Paz. Their last sight of their mother prior to intake included her urging them to deny everything and come back home.

There's no quick fix for suffering like Sophia's. For a long time, she held herself back. After several months, her self-esteem had improved, but it disappeared when she delivered her baby boy, Carlos.

Sophia had just celebrated her twelfth birthday.

At first, she didn't seem to love little Carlos at all. She was angry – not loud angry, but moody and sullen. My brother, George, and his wife, Mary, were serving as houseparents at that time. Mary did what she always did and loved Sophia no matter what. I know this helped Sophia's heart soften. But after the nursing process ended when Carlos was maybe six months old, others could take care of the baby. Finally, Sophia had the chance to be a child again.

We raised Carlos to know Sophia was his mom, but Sophia tried to keep the relationship from growing close. As time went by, however, she did more and more things with her son, sitting with him at meals and watching out for him on the playground. But her anger remained – and so did that faraway look in her eyes, the one that told me God had more work to do.

At Sophia's quinceañera, something changed. We try to make as much as we can of these fifteenth-birthday parties, bringing in fancy dresses and making sure the birthday girl has plenty of gifts. For Sophia's party, we even hired a small Christian mariachi band.

Sophia's mother hadn't come to the party. She wanted nothing to do with Sophia, especially since the boyfriend was now in jail. She sometimes visited her sons but never spoke to Sophia or Carlos.

Pastor Lujan gave a short message straight to Sophia as she

sat in a chair the other girls had decorated with tulle and flowers. When he finished, he asked me to pray over her.

I walked forward and placed my hands on her shoulders. I meant to pray a simple prayer, but God had something else in mind. He poured His words through me: "The past is gone. I see you as who you are: a lovely young woman." Her tears streamed as I continued: "You have a new future ahead. Acknowledge Him in all your ways and He will make your paths straight." I prayed for what seemed like hours. And as I did, a holy hush fell on the party.

Sophia arose from that chair with a new look in her eyes, a new smile on her face. Today, she lives in a nearby town where she has a special scholarship to help her finish her high school diploma. She works part-time and is learning the skills that, one day, will allow her to bring Carlos out of the orphanage.

Our Sophia has, by God's grace, walked away from the unspeakable and out of the dust.

CHAPTER 5

Love Never Fails

I don't want anyone to think my siblings and I had a terrible childhood. None of us would say that. Our growing up was different, yes, but our parents loved us, and we knew it. Even with Dad's strange way of thinking, he always kept his respect for God and his country.

Whenever we traveled (which seemed like most of the time), Dad kept a Bible in the window behind the car's back seat. No matter how crowded things got, he never allowed us to put anything on top of it. "We have to give honor to God's Word," he said.

Dad wasn't the only one who taught us respect for God, though. Mom tried to see that we got to church everywhere we lived. By the time she got all us kids ready, she didn't often attend services herself, but she made sure we went whenever we could.

By the time Rada turned nine and I, ten, we would find a church ourselves and drag our little brothers and sister along. We loved to go to Sunday school too. One summer, we attended a church that offered a Bible Drill program. I look back on those months of memorizing verses as one of the best summers of my childhood.

Mom also read a chapter from the Bible aloud every night. We might be sleeping in the car or sitting around a campfire, but she made sure to read that chapter. If we had a house, all of us kids would pile on Mom and Dad's bed as she read. As a result, we all grew up knowing about Jesus and His importance in our lives. And we all learned about grace in our own way.

It took me a while to grasp this lesson. One summer, when I was about eleven or twelve, we started going to a church where they talked about getting saved. I'd go down to the altar and cry my heart out, asking Jesus to come in.

This particular church believed you weren't saved unless you spoke in tongues, so I kept trying, but nothing happened. *Maybe I'm not really saved*, I thought. And I'd go forward once again. I'd get home and feel good about my spiritual condition – until something happened. Maybe the boys would stomp through the house in their muddy boots. I'd chase them out with a broom and feel like I had to start all over again. For a while, it seemed like I got saved every week.

At that point in my life, I knew Jesus. I'd accepted Him to the level of my understanding. But I was almost thirty years old before I had a true picture of God's grace. I can look back now and see how He often poured it out on our family.

Sometimes, His grace came through miracles. Our family still talks about the "miracle tire." One night on a twisty mountain road with all our belongings piled on top of the car as usual, a tire blew. Dad bumped to the side of the road to examine the flat.

"It's bad," he reported. "All torn up and cut." He jacked up the car, making sure we all stayed inside. "Elsie," he told Mom, "Don't let the kids out. They'll get killed."

He took the tire and trudged down the hill, his pockets

empty. As he left, all of us kids cried. I don't remember if we prayed or not, but I do remember we all had a deep concern for Dad and our ruined tire.

Dad went to the first garage he saw and showed the tire to the mechanic on duty. "Can you fix it?" he asked.

The man looked at the tire. "It's all chewed up," he said, shaking his head. "There's nothing I can do. Why don't you check with the garage across the street?"

Dad took their advice. Again, he asked for the mechanic and showed him the flat, ready to begin his spiel. But to his surprise, the tire now looked normal. No longer destroyed, it looked solid, whole, and ready to use again. God fixed the tire while Dad walked across the street. All the mechanic had to do was put it back on the rim.

Dad came back and told us the story right away. "I can't believe it. I didn't know what I was going to do," he said, adding, "I didn't have a cent. Only God could have healed that tire."

Dad put the rubber miracle back on the car and away we went. Our circumstances hadn't changed, but we all had new hope. God used the tire to show us He was still taking care of us.

He took care of us through people too. Everywhere we went, godly women brought us clothes and food or ministered in other ways. As a young girl, these women meant so much to me. I can't remember their faces, but I do remember their attitudes, their joy, and how much they talked about Jesus. I decided I wanted to be like them someday.

I think about that when groups of volunteers come to minister to our children. I tell them, "They may not remember you, but they'll remember your message of kindness and relate it to Jesus."

The roots of my own call to missions began with acts of kindness. After our family was on the move again, our car broke down near Gallup, New Mexico. When the engine quit in the middle of the night, we sat on the side of the road until daybreak.

A young couple came along in a pickup just after sunrise. They turned out to be missionaries who worked with the Native Americans there. "Come with us," they said. "You can stay in our home, and we know some people who can fix your car."

For the next few days, as we waited on the repair work, I couldn't stop watching the missionary wife. She was young, pretty, involved with kids, and in love with Jesus. She and her husband had adopted a three-year-old Native American boy, and they were caring for several other children too – broken kids, the kind no one else wanted.

Their adopted son had a caved-in chest. When he was a baby, his birth mother dropped him during a bar fight. Someone stepped on him and damaged the bones in his chest, but doctors believed they would one day reshape themselves.

For the first time, I had the chance to see God's love at work from the missionaries' side. They showed kindness to everyone they met in spite of the pain that surrounded them. They had little, but they shared much, with joy and love for both God and people. At only twelve years old, the Lord gave me the privilege of seeing His love displayed through their ministry to hurt and abandoned children.

Before we left, I told the young wife that I wanted to go to Bible school and become a missionary too. She didn't laugh or say, "You're too young," or "Wait until you grow up." Instead, she gave me the address of the school where she and her husband had gone. "Keep following the Lord," she urged.

We left Gallup after a few days, and I never saw her again. But God used her to plant the seed of missionary service in my heart. For years, it lay dormant. And none of us expected it to take root and grow the way it did.

As I explained earlier, my brothers, sisters, and I had an

unusual childhood, but we also had some special benefits. Mom read to us with inflection and great emphasis, from the Bible and other books, too. Six of us – including me – are dyslexic, but Mom instilled in us a love of reading and books. In the car, she spelled out words, called out math problems, and talked with us about life.

"Your father is sick and doesn't always know what he's doing," Mom would say. "But when you grow up, you should stay in one place and get a job. Always pay your bills, and always be honest." Mom expected great things from all seven of us. When someone knocked us down, she expected us to get back up. "No matter how hard things get," she told us, "better times are on the way."

Mom also knew how to forgive. Over the years, she forgave Dad over and over again. "If you don't forgive people, it will make you old and wrinkled," she told us, and to this day, I believe her. When she died at age seventy-five, she still had smooth, beautiful skin.

Growing up with Dad made me realize that people can't give you what they don't have. His illness caused him to move in and out of a fantasy. Once I understood that, I could forgive him for all the jobs and moves. He gave us what he had – love, admiration, and a sense of family unity. When I think back, I remember his pride in our smallest accomplishments. He showed off my childish pictures even to strangers as though they were great works of art. He praised all of us kids for our accomplishments and instilled within us the confidence that we could do anything if only we tried.

At a young age, my brother George showed great mechanical ability. At only about eight years old, he took a lawnmower engine apart and put it back together. Dad beamed with pride. "Can you believe that boy?"

Today, there isn't an engine George can't diagnose and repair.

He even serves in a ministry at his church that helps fix cars for widows and others who need help.

Too often we demand what we want from people even when they don't have it to give. But only Jesus can fulfill all our expectations. When we love without condition, we free ourselves as well as others.

Don't waste your pain.

When I look back on my childhood, I remember the good. I love to tell people, "Don't waste your pain."

God hasn't wasted a single bit of mine. Everywhere I go, I meet people who have suffered some of the same hard things I did. They trust me because they know I understand. That opens the door for me to share the same good news that helped bring me out of the dust.

Out of the Dust: Fred and George Miller

I guess you could say my brothers Fred and George, like the rest of us Miller kids, understand life in the dust. "We lived in very poor areas, very similar to Pacasmayo. The terrain was similar, and we were raised with all different kinds of people," Fred explains. "When we see these kids playing in dirt and stuff, with no real toys other than imaginary or homemade toys, that's how we were raised." He adds, "We see ourselves there."

Like me, Fred sees the good in our childhood. "As we were growing up, many people helped us out." He pauses and adds, "We don't remember their names now, but God's angels would come through and help us. That's why we want to do things to help these kids."

George also sees the past through a positive lens. "I tell people I had an excellent childhood. I enjoyed my brothers and sisters."

He adds, "The things we went through – they gave us a close-ness. The way we were raised gave us a deep love for each other. Any of us would help the other one out and be happy to do it. The way we were raised is a God-story, and I thank Him for it."

God could have shown us kids we could identify with any-where, but he chose to do it in Peru. As Fred says, "When we see little kids playing with rocks, sticks – all sweaty, dirty, and playing imaginary games, kids who don't have enough to eat – we see ourselves. It's a delight to have God use us, because He's working through us. And through our upbringing, we learned it's not the house or fancy furniture, but people who make a home."

I don't think any of us regret it. And I know we'd do it all again.

CHAPTER 6

More Growing

I n May of 1958, our family moved before the school year ended – this time to Albuquerque. There, Rada got scarlet fever, and I got my first real job. Only fourteen, I worked as a carhop at The Farmer's Daughter, a small drive-in restaurant on Route 66. "I'm sixteen," I told the owners. For some reason, they believed me.

In this family-owned business, I learned the basics of time and motion. To mix up a milkshake, for example, I shouldn't keep crossing the kitchen to gather the needed supplies. Instead, I should get them all in one trip.

That put a landmark in my mind. From then on, I started thinking things through and planning the most efficient way to accomplish them. That comes in handy on the mission field, where I often put people, needs, and supplies together.

Every payday, Dad came by the restaurant to pick up my check. But I wanted to give it to Mom instead. With Dad, I never knew what would happen. We argued, but most of the time, he left with the check.

He let me keep my tax refunds, though. I used the first one to buy a sewing machine and the second to buy a car out in

Temple City, California, where our family moved next. It was an old clunker, but it suited me fine.

By then, I had plenty of driving experience because we had two family cars, an old Buick and a step-down Hudson. And, still fourteen years old, I drove the Buick all the way from Albuquerque to Los Angeles during our move. "Don't look to either side," Dad said. "Just keep your eyes on the road. You'll do fine." And I did.

In Temple City, we all started school a little late. Whenever Dad decided to move, he never took time to collect our school records. Our new school sent for them, but when they arrived, we were well into the academic year. At that point, even though the transcripts revealed that we hadn't finished the previous school year, the administration decided not to move us back.

We all remember our time in Temple City as the year Bobby got burned. In the fall, Carol began kindergarten, so Mom got a job in the secretarial pool at Republic Supply Company. One Saturday, all four brothers were outside flipping matches. Somehow, one managed to spin right into a gallon bottle of gasoline Dad kept for the lawnmower.

In a flash, the bottle caught fire. Twelve-year-old Bobby ran to pour the flaming liquid onto the ground, but it splashed onto his pant legs instead. Screaming, he ran behind the house. Our brother Art ran the other way to a place where a dripping faucet left a muddy spot in our yard. As Bobby came around the side of the house, Art tackled him, rolled him in the mud, and put out the fire.

Mom and Dad rushed out to see what was happening. Later, Mom said she thought Bobby's socks had fallen down around his ankles. Before she could say anything, she realized the truth. The wrinkled lumps above his shoes weren't socks, but all that was left of the skin on his shins and ankles.

"I'm okay, I'm okay," our tough little brother repeated. But Mom and Dad rushed him off to the nearest emergency room.

Because of Mom's job and medical benefits, Bobby could have the skin graft operations he needed. Only God's grace could have provided both the resources to save his legs and the strength to endure the horrific procedure.

Once the hospital released him, Bobby had a long recovery period, so we stayed put longer than usual. To trade off on nursing duty, Rada stayed home from school one day and I the next. Dad had left for parts unknown, and Mom needed to keep her job.

After two months, the school investigated all the absences. They sent out a home teacher when they found out about Bobby's burns. With such intensive tutoring, he finally learned to read. Because of our dyslexia, most of us Miller kids struggled with reading. But that year, Bobby earned straight A's. And we finished the year in the same school where we'd started for the first time ever.

The home teacher also knew about a camp for burn victims and arranged for Bobby to go. A scholarship covered his registration costs, but we had to deal with his packing list.

Of course we had no money to buy things like deodorant, a toothbrush, or toothpaste. In our family, these were extras, not essentials. How could Bobby get to camp?

Rada offered, "You can take my toothbrush."

"Mrs. Harris asked me to cut her grass," Art spoke up. "You can have what she pays me." One by one, we all chipped in until Bobby had everything he needed.

That summer, we all went to camp in a way, because our brother took along our love, our support, and more than a few of our belongings.

Once Bobby finished healing, our family was on the move again. After three short hops between California and Arizona, we landed in a small Arizona town. Here Rada and I, along with my brand-new boyfriend, Wayne, attended a Holiness church. Almost right away, I went door to door to share Jesus. Wayne, Rada, and I started a youth group and rounded up the kids. I went back to learn more every Sunday. For the first time in my life, I was truly on fire for the Lord.

During this same time, I sensed God calling me to preach. I felt like Moses — scared to death. But just like Moses, once I started, the words flowed. I know now that the Lord was preparing me to take the gospel to Central and South America years later.

It seemed no time passed until we were moving again — first, back to California, and then to Denver a few months later. I was struggling more than ever, mostly because of my relationship with Wayne.

Yes, my boyfriend had moved with us. My parents never knew it, but I felt pulled in two directions: walking with the Lord and walking in the flesh.

Somewhere in all the moves our family dropped out of church. But Jesus remained my Savior and hope, and I never quit loving Him. I decided the only way to straighten out the wrong in my dating relationship was to get married.

Wayne knew how to work and keep a job. That made him especially attractive to a girl who grew up the way I did. *This is a man I can go through life with*, I thought. I turned eighteen on November 6, and we planned our wedding for New Year's Eve.

Tim, my sister Rada, and I went out together right after my birthday. Rada had just turned seventeen, and Wayne was teaching her to drive. We lived in government housing, and during this, my senior year, I had a job at Woolworth's. Wayne had his own apartment by then, although he still spent plenty of time with our family.

The roads were icy that afternoon, so Rada's driving lesson

didn't last long. Wayne sat up front so he could instruct her. He was a patient teacher, but the slippery roads scared her and she soon asked him to drive.

Wayne turned the ice into a game, adding in a few extra slips and slides along the way. We wound up high in the mountains, laughing and carrying on. We found an almost-deserted truck stop and scraped together enough money to buy pie and coffee, a special treat.

I felt like Moses – scared to death.

The fun ended when we arrived back home. It was only six o'clock, but Dad thought we'd stayed out too late. "When's this wedding gonna be?" he screamed. "You should've been home long ago!"

That did it. I walked into my bedroom, grabbed a few school-books, and told my mother, "I'm leaving. I'm moving out."

"You can't!"

"Mom, I'm eighteen. I'm going." I rested my hand on the doorknob. "Just don't say anything to Dad." Wayne and I left in his car.

I took some of my savings and rented a large room with a kitchen in one corner. A policeman went home with me the next day to get the rest of my things.

Wayne and I soon decided to elope. At seventeen, he looked like a ten-year-old. But somehow, he got a phony I.D. card, and we took off. Rumor had it that you could get married in New Mexico without much hassle, so that's where we headed.

We made it to Taos sometime after midnight and slept in the car. Early in the morning, we took ourselves and our documents in to the rickety old building that housed the justice of the peace.

"Well, I don't know about this," the official drawled as he looked over the paperwork. "Got anybody to verify his age?"

"My mother." I spoke almost too quickly. "He's lived with our family for over a year."

"Best get her on the phone then."

I went to the pay phone in the corner and, in what I hoped was a confident whisper, explained the situation. "Mom, it's me." I paused. "I'm not coming home until I'm married, and I'm not getting married until you tell this man that Wayne's twenty-one."

The entire town must have heard her shriek "*What*?" But she agreed to cooperate. My newly-mature fiancé and I went to the justice of the peace's home for our wedding. But first I dressed myself in the white gown and veil stuffed into the trunk of Wayne's big old car. We recited the vows, signed the papers, and received an unwanted wedding present in the form of a young bobcat thrust upon us as we left.

Dizzy with adventure and the excitement of achieving our goal, we drove all the way back to Denver to spend our honeymoon night in my rented room.

We awoke the next morning to someone pounding on the door. Dad heard about our wedding and showed up to wish us the best.

"Well, you've done it. Congratulations!" That was Dad, switching from anger to acceptance in no time.

I remember thinking right away that I needed to help with the kids' Christmas. I used my Woolworth's discount to buy new sweaters for all my brothers and a huge doll, three feet tall, for my baby sister. For the first time, I could give everyone in our family a present.

My newlywed life was good, but my missionary calling melted into the background as I focused on building a life with Wayne. I didn't notice at the time, but I was the only one trying.

Out of the Dust:
Arada's Story

I'm only a year and nineteen days younger than Avis, so for me, she's always been there. If there had been no Avis, my life would have been so boring.

I remember one time when we were living in a house with a little corn crib off to one side. Avis was maybe ten years old, but she put benches and a pulpit inside and made us kids sit in there while she preached.

I also remember starting at a brand-new school in Sunny Slope, Arizona. We were walking to the bus stop for the first time when Avis said, "Radee, this is a new school. If we tried, we could really become leaders."

At the same time, I was thinking, "Wow. I hope I get on the right bus to come home." That shows the difference between us.

It's hard to explain what it was like to grow up in our family. Sometimes it was embarrassing. Mom and Dad would join a church, and before we knew it, Dad would start mooching off church members. As a child, when you go through that, you make up your mind: "I don't want to live like this when I grow up."

But the orphans at Casa de Paz don't have any way to provide for themselves. At least in our situation, Mom and Dad were around most of the time. A lot of these kids have been hurt, beaten, and abandoned. It's beyond anything we ever experienced. But Avis has a heart for them.

Our background gives all of us a special compassion for others. When you've been hungry, you don't forget. When Avis sees an orphan without food or a girl passed out on the street, she knows what it feels like.

We all know what it's like to be a child and be alone. We know what it feels like to be on the taking end. It makes you not want to be a taker. As an adult, you want to give.

CHAPTER 7

Beyond "I Do"

I was pregnant almost right away. Wayne had a job with a plastic extrusion company, and I was still working at Woolworth's. Mom, Dad, and the kids made another one of their sudden moves only a month later. They ended up in California while Wayne and I stayed in Denver.

What should have been a happy time became anything but. I was living without family nearby for the first time ever, and I had no warm clothes for the long Colorado winter. I wanted to finish high school, but once the administration learned of my pregnancy, they refused to let me attend. *Why didn't we wait a few more months?*

After Wayne's paychecks began bouncing, we decided to move back to his hometown in Arizona. There, at least, we'd be warm.

We lived with his Cherokee grandmother. Years of diabetes left her mind confused, but she had a great love for the Lord, for people, and for her little church.

I remember waking up in the night to find her baking pies or cooking beans and rice. "The church is having a fellowship supper," she would say. The food was wonderful, but there was no fellowship supper planned. We started locking the refrigerator to keep her from making unneeded meals.

I was excited about the baby, but Wayne pressured me to have an abortion. Then he moved to California, leaving me with his grandmother. "You can come after I get settled," he said. Almost right away, his cousins (two girls and a guy) helped him get a night job with Farmer John's Meat Company.

I loved caring for Grandma, but I missed my husband and family. About halfway through the pregnancy, I took a bus out to La Puente to join my husband, who was living with my parents. We rented a cute little house. I was excited about fixing it up, and Wayne seemed to have accepted the idea of fatherhood at last.

But the cousin connection was nothing but trouble. They were all older than Wayne and took him out drinking after work. I was busy playing mommy-to-be while the girls swarmed him. He was living the good life, only I didn't realize how good – or how bad – it was.

Our sweet baby girl, Tia, arrived near the end of August. I found myself pregnant again before she turned two, with my marriage crumbling around me. Wayne and his cousins went to the bars almost every night after work. When he found out about the pregnancy, something snapped.

I knew I had to provide for my children and me, so I borrowed money from my sister and bought into a custom bra business. Right after little Mark arrived, Wayne left for several months. But about the time our son turned six months old, he returned, ready to try again.

His next job offer was at an ammunition dump near Kansas City, where we moved just after Mark turned one. Wayne later worked as an apprentice meat cutter. But he still seemed to find other women more appealing than his wife.

The rest of my family was living in nearby Lawrence, Kansas.

I had earned my high school diploma by taking continuing education classes after Tia was born. Now it was my brother Fred's turn. He was a senior when Dad came home with a familiar announcement: "We have to move."

"I can't, Dad," Fred told him. "Graduation's only a few months away. Can't we go after that?"

In Dad's mind, a high school diploma was nothing to wait around for. Fred decided to stay in Lawrence in a friend's tiny attic room, and our family left the state without him. He lived on packaged soup and day-old bread but kept studying and working at his part-time job. He would be the first from our family to graduate from regular high school.

One day, the principal called Fred into his office. "I'm sorry, son, but we can't let you walk in the graduation line looking like that."

"What do you mean?"

"You've got to get a haircut and a new pair of shoes."

Fred looked down at the duct tape he'd used to reattach the sole to one of his shoes. Didn't that look better than letting it flap up and down? And yes, his hair hung over his collar, but he had no money for a haircut. It was all he could do to pay his rent and buy enough food to survive.

When Fred told me about his chat with the principal, I knew what I had to do. Wayne and I didn't have much money, but I sent enough for a haircut and shoes. I couldn't let my brother miss his high school graduation. Mom, Rada, and I beamed from the stands a few weeks later as Fred received his diploma.

My bra business did well and I soon had forty women working for me. I then became a district manager, and Wayne became a journeyman meat cutter. We bought a house. However, he still stayed out all night at least twice a week, and his girlfriends kept calling him at home. On the outside, we were a sweet young couple, but on the inside, everything was broken.

During this time, the kids and I attended a Nazarene church. I always viewed God the way I did my natural father: good to have around, but not good to trust. I depended only on myself.

Our church was close to the Nazarene seminary, and I went to a Sunday school class with lots of young seminary couples. Our rotating Bible study group met in different homes every week. I loved our yearlong examination of *The Late, Great Planet Earth* by Hal Lindsey, my first exposure to Bible prophecy.

As we studied the book, I understood that God has a plan for all time. I also began reading *The Living Bible*, especially on the nights when Wayne didn't come home. The Lord was opening my eyes to the truth, but I still didn't have a total commitment. I thought I could be a Christian under my own power – until something happened that took away my strength.

I'm a good girl. Bad things aren't supposed to happen to me.

At first, I didn't realize I was ill. But soon I couldn't get out of bed, and doctors diagnosed me with pernicious anemia. Vitamin B-12 shots helped, but only for a while. Tests showed I had many more white blood cells than red, and I stayed in bed for months, growing weaker and weaker.

I felt so isolated. I itched all over and had unbearable pain. My eyebrows and much of my hair fell out. *What's happening? If I die, who will take care of my children?*

I couldn't count on Wayne, although for now, he was trying to help. I started making deals with God, but I stayed sick. Very sick.

What's wrong? I'm a good girl. Bad things aren't supposed to happen to me.

I pleaded with God. "Lord, you know I don't understand. And no matter what we do, I'm not getting any better." I added my most serious words yet. "If you're not going to heal me, take me. Tonight. Please. Just go ahead and take me. I'm ready."

At midnight, I waited. Nothing happened.

When I didn't die, I yelled. "I'm nothing," I told the Lord. "I'm worthless! Why would you even want me? Live or die; it's up to you."

Finally, I gave up. I couldn't get out of bed, let alone fix my situation. In my mind, you had to *do* something to be worth something. And I could do nothing.

That's when the visions began. For about two weeks, every time the pain became unbearable, I saw a bubble at the foot of my bed with Jesus inside. When the pain came, so did Jesus and the powerful sense of His presence. I had felt so alone, but now, I understood: *He is with me.*

I remembered the Bible said He has laid all our sickness, pain, sins, shame, and guilt upon Him. *He knows. He feels my hurt and isolation.* I now looked forward to the pain, because it meant Jesus would come.

One evening I awoke from a nap. It was almost dark, and I could hear Wayne, the kids, the television, and the babysitter, who was getting ready to leave. A piercing sound with deep vibrations filled the room, growing louder and louder. "Has death come?" I asked God.

"Not now, later." As soon as He spoke, the sound decreased. *I want to go with Him, but He says "Not now."*

I felt the noise draining out of me along with my pain. *He's healing me!* I fell asleep, exhausted.

When I woke up, it was morning. I didn't feel healed, just sick. And I didn't want to take any more pills. I staggered out to the kitchen to turn on the water and garbage disposal. I dumped bottle after bottle of medicine down the drain, until the disposal started spitting the pills back out.

"What are you doing?" Wayne shouted, running in to shut everything off. "You're crazy!"

Wayne shoved me, still in my pajamas, into the car. My

doctor was out of town, so we drove to another specialist, who ran blood tests right away. We waited for the report.

Pretty soon I heard the doctor talking to Wayne as though I wasn't there. "The only thing wrong with your wife is her addiction to pain medication and other drugs. You can put her in [a local rehab center] and dry her out, or you can take her home and watch her."

I could hardly believe him. *Addicted? Me?* But he continued: "She doesn't have pernicious anemia. I don't know what happened, but it's gone. These medicines are the only problem now."

After the doctor explained the withdrawal process, Wayne chose to take me home. Expecting the worst, I went to bed and slept for three days.

When I woke up, I didn't have the fever, the chills, or the other withdrawal symptoms the doctor described. God had healed my addictions too.

From then on I knew that one day I had an appointment with God. "Not now, later," He had said, and I knew I would keep doing my best. But I was still trying to live the Christian life in my own power. And I needed many more lessons before I would surrender all.

During the worst phase of my illness, I sold my share of the bra business to Rachel, who had started out as one of my trainees but quickly became both friend and colleague. She also helped me in my Christian walk and was one of my strongest supporters.

As my health improved, I went to work again, this time for Minnetonka Labs. I helped put their makeup into drugstores and trained other women to display and sell it. Every three weeks, I flew to Minnesota for another training session or pep rally. It was a hectic life, but I loved it.

I found out Wayne was having another affair and wanted to get him out of Kansas. He agreed to try living in California once more. Rada and her husband were buying a cactus farm in Valley Center, and we planned to go into business with them.

California was fine. The wholesale cactus business was fine. But our marriage? Not so fine.

After only three months in California, Wayne began an affair with a neighbor. We'd gone to counseling off and on for years, but I finally realized things weren't going to work out. As one of my Christian friends said, "Avis, you can't be married all by yourself."

That hit me hard. We'd been married eleven years, but my husband hadn't lived like a married man for at least ten. I made the decision to do what he'd already done and end our marriage.

I didn't know it, but even these struggles prepared me for the mission field. Jesus identified with my heartache, and one day, I would identify with other women in theirs.

Out of the Dust: Pastor William Collaci Cecairos's Story

I've been a pastor here in Pacasmayo for only a few years, and marriages are a large part of my ministry. Before that, I was a business executive in Lima. But I kept visiting here and seeing everything God was doing.

When I first came here to visit, I saw a man kicking a woman just outside the church. I went over to him, but he grabbed the woman by the neck and left. That hurt my heart and helped me decide to serve here.

I want to be in the hearts of my people. They're different than in any other part of Peru because they feel distant from God. They come to church, they leave church, and they go do whatever they feel like. I want to change the hearts of the families and teenagers because we need to change this generation.

When I came here, I found so many men with more than one woman. They would marry one, have two or three children, then leave and find someone new. Around here, that's normal. I would talk with the man, and he'd say, "I can't leave my wife." And the woman said things like, "I love him. I need him." So many families were broken.

We've had three weddings since I've been here, so we are helping restore marriages. I pray every day to be in the people's hearts.

My words don't have power, but the Word of God has the power to change their lives and mine. And I use the Word of God.

CHAPTER 8

Desperation and Deliverance

I'd reached the point of desperation, but nobody knew.
That evening in 1977, as I lay sobbing on my bed, something changed inside.

No, I thought. *I'm not going to do this anymore. I've cried
enough. I've already got the name. Why not play the game?*

Divorcee. I hated that word, but it described me. Maybe I
married too soon after my marriage to Wayne finally ended.
Or maybe I married the wrong man. *If Dean doesn't want me,
I just don't care anymore.*

I met Dean, my second husband, not long after my marriage
to Wayne broke up. I was living on nine acres in Valley Center,
California, where our family owned the cactus nursery. Dean,
who lived nearby, heard about me from a friend. He came by
the nursery, pretending to be interested in cacti.

It didn't take long to figure out his real interest. And it didn't
take long – only a few months of dating – for us to get married.
But after less than a year of marriage, he had asked me to leave.

Our plan to put our two families together just wasn't working. On top of that, Dean was drinking, running around with

other women, and drinking some more. He asked me to move out because "You make me feel guilty."

No kidding. At first, I took the kids and went back to my own trailer home. Then we moved to Arizona, closer to more of my family.

That's where I lay that night, ready for the dating game. I sat up, shimmied my shoulders, fluffed my hair, and unfastened my top button. *What's the point of being good, anyway? I've been good my whole life, and look where's it's gotten me. Time for a new plan. Mine.*

I looked in the mirror. *I just want to have a good time.*

I continued my preparations when a voice interrupted. "Go ahead. Try to make yourself happy."

What? God must have known I needed more than a voice, because the scene played out like a movie on the screen of my mind. A woman, fixing up a house for her kids and a man. The house looked beautiful, but soon the man got bored, and another came. The same scene repeated itself with another man, another house, another man, and another house. At the end, I saw the woman. Old. Wrinkled. Used-up. Worn-out.

Old. Wrinkled. Used-up. Worn-out.

I was the woman.

I knew God was offering me a choice: His way or my way; life or death. No more playing around with Christianity while keeping my options open. No more one foot in, one foot out.

I spoke to God as directly as He did to me. "With my children, without my children. With my husband, without a husband. Jesus, I'll follow you 'til the day I die."

What was different about this from all the other times I gave God my life? For several years, I'd considered myself a Christian. So what made the change?

Three things: trust, commitment, and dependence. I was no longer trusting in myself or my own ability to be good. Instead,

I was placing my faith in Christ and making a commitment to Him. I found myself suddenly and completely dependent on Jesus and the price He paid for me. Out of the dust of not one but two marriages, I was giving up the control I gripped for so long.

A wave of total peace washed over me. *Dependent on Christ.* Who knew I would find such power there?

At almost the same time, God was dealing with Dean, whose drinking problem had torn us apart. Back in Valley Center, he was busy working as an avocado buyer during the day and closing down the bars at night.

One awful evening, he passed out and fell out the door of his truck on the side of a dirt road. He had somehow put the vehicle in neutral, lights on and motor running. The scenario had happened before, but this time was different. There in the dust, God brought Dean a mind-movie too. His entire life passed before his eyes, and he was sick – so sick he believed he was dying.

For days, one thought ran through his head: *Where's it all going to wind up?* He couldn't escape it. *Where's it all going to wind up?*

There on the side of the road, Dean faced the same choice I had: life or death. He cried out, "God, I'm sorry for the mess I've made of my life. I know I can't fix it. Only you can do that."

Dean pleaded for the strength to trust Jesus. He never took another drink of alcohol from then on. Out of the dust, God began building something beautiful.

Trust, commitment, and dependence. The elements that brought me new life did the same thing for my husband, although I didn't realize anything had changed.

Dean and I had already endured several months of separation. Once a month, we met near the Arizona border to handle paperwork and other legal matters. We would eat, sign documents, and go our separate ways.

At our next meeting, I noticed Dean didn't order a drink. "Why not?" I asked. "You're shaking. What's going on?"

He paused a long moment before telling me he hadn't had a drink in a week. He wasn't ready to share his story, though. "I can't promise you anything, because I can't even promise myself I won't drink before the day is over," he said. "It's a second-by-second, minute-by-minute situation."

I stared at the man I thought I knew. He looked old, gray, and tired – but sober. "I'm not ready to talk about it," he said again. "We'll just have to wait and see."

Dean showed up at my Arizona home a month later and moved us back to Valley Center. I could hardly believe it. God had restored what I thought was forever lost. And I had done nothing to manage, fix, or control it.

Dean and I were back together, but life wasn't easy. He had a tough time leaving his alcohol habit and still suffered from DTs (*delirium tremens*, one symptom of alcohol withdrawal). With God's help, he hung in there, and we started putting our kids back together: my Tia (now fourteen) and Mark (eleven); and Dean's Glen (eighteen), Cindy (sixteen), and Cleta (ten), although Cleta only lived with us part-time.

Blending two sets of children from two different backgrounds was one of the hardest jobs I've ever had. But God had some advice: "Spend a little bit of individual time with each child every day."

The kids didn't realize I was doing this, and at first, it only felt awkward. But the more time we spent together, the more the conversation flowed.

We also began what we called family meetings. Our rule said that everyone had a few minutes to speak without interruptions.

We could all voice our opinions or grievances, but Dean and I had the final say.

Little by little, we became a family. Of course, we still faced challenges, partly because we were living in the place where our problems started. So we made the decision to move to Arkansas.

Dean always talked about this state like it was the Promised Land, a place of good, clean living. We decided the change would give our family a great new start.

We moved in April of 1979, rented a house in Prairie Grove, and bought a bulldozer. Dean started getting jobs right away. He dug ponds, made dams, built chicken pads, dug dirt roads, and cleared land. He and that 'dozer could do almost anything.

We saw God's faithfulness at work that first winter. Our payments on the bulldozer were more than $600 a month, but Dean insisted we pay our tithe to the church we attended. As the bookkeeper, I knew we didn't have enough to live on through the winter and keep up our payments. But numbers don't limit God. We made it through with money to spare. Before long, we were clearing land to build a house.

Although Dean no longer drank, he struggled with his nerves. A broken piece of equipment would overwhelm him, and he had to come find me. I listened until he ran out of steam, then asked, "How do we fix it? Where can we get the parts?" I had to be available to my husband at moments like this, so I didn't think about looking for work.

At the same time, God grew in me a desire to minister to the local youth. I wanted to pick up all the neighbor kids and take them to church, and I wanted to go to Sunday school, not just worship services. But Dean wasn't ready. Not yet, anyway.

As I pondered this problem one day, God spoke: "You take care of my business, and I'll take care of yours." I knew what He meant. If I'd pick up the neighbor kids and take them to Sunday school, He'd take care of Dean.

And he did – in a much better way than I could have. God gently guided him through the healing process until one day he came with me to Sunday school, church, and almost everything else. He even joined a Christian gospel music group.

Dean's deep baritone voice sang his testimony in churches all over the southwestern part of the United States. His favorite song, Bill and Gloria Gaither's "Thanks to Calvary (I Don't Live Here Anymore)," seemed the perfect description of his life story.

I remember this as a time of great healing. I spent many hours alone tending my plants, grateful for God's presence, provision, and abundance. As I gardened, I carried on a running conversation with Him. Somewhere in this time, I learned that an attitude of gratitude brings His presence. And His presence brings the joy of the Lord, our strength.

God allowed me to stay home, give my children needed support, and help my husband with his bulldozer business. Dean said my job was to keep the garden and raise the kids. He had a firm belief in not spending beyond our means, so we paid off our mortgage in only eight years.

God kept nurturing me, increasing my desire to teach young people about Jesus. Another woman and I took over the youth department at New Sulphur Free Will Baptist Church, and with His help, the program grew to fifty kids.

Throughout this faith journey, God grew me. Everywhere I went, I took kids along, and we told everyone about Jesus. I participated in Bible Study Fellowship (BSF) for five years, which proved to be a wonderful grounding in Scripture. For two of those years, I helped in the children's fellowship.

My new Bible knowledge gave me a new courage. Before long, I was teaching the teen class along with missionary women, adults, and Sunday night services.

I didn't know it, but God was preparing me not only for the next step, but for several steps down the road.

Out of the Dust:
Pilar Murrugara Flores's Story

Sister Avis has a true heart for women. I first met her nine or ten years ago. She was having a women's meeting at a neighbor's house, and I wanted to see what was happening. I found her preaching to the women there. I talked to her afterward, and she was very nice. I went to another meeting with these women and invited many of my friends.

Before long, Avis told us she was about to buy the land to build a church, and now we have it. This place was only trash, but now, it's wonderful. I never could have imagined this beautiful place here.

Before I met Avis, I didn't have a personal relationship with Jesus. I had many idols in my home. I put candles around them, and whenever I needed something, I asked the idols to help me.

When the church was first built, I didn't come right away. But Sister Avis kept visiting me. I remember her saying, "I need you in the church!" I wasn't sure if I should listen, but one Sunday, I decided to come anyway.

It was a beautiful morning, and the message Sister Avis gave touched me. I decided to ask Jesus to come into my heart, and my life changed. Now I pray as soon as I wake up and all day long. My husband and my sons came to church too, and all except the youngest have been baptized.

Our family life is much better now than before. My husband has stopped drinking, and he doesn't hit or abuse me. He and I are always talking about the Lord, and my sons follow God too. I thank Him for this change in my family. Sister Avis and the church are a blessing to many so they can come and have the opportunity to have Him in their hearts.

CHAPTER 9

Teaching and Learning

The more I learned, the more I taught. Probably because I had teenage children at the time, I found myself connecting with other teenagers too.

I remember picking up the football players, including my son, Mark, from school on Wednesday nights for the twelve-mile drive out in the country to Bible study at our church. Mark and I had a great relationship, and on those drives he and his friends felt free to talk. They asked me questions about almost anything: sex, drugs, schooling, and life in general. So few of them had a trusted adult to talk to, and so much learning happened on Wednesday night drives in that old Cadillac.

I wrote on a blackboard when I taught the youth Bible study, but at first, that scared me. I knew my dyslexia would show itself, and I expected no mercy from the kids. But my desire to teach them about Jesus helped me push past my concern.

Whenever I taught, I held up the Bible and said, "God wants me to teach you what's in this book. There are some big words in it, and I can't pronounce them. But He's given me a good understanding of what they mean, so when I write something on the board, I want Chad [the smartest boy in the class] to make sure I spell and pronounce it correctly."

About fifty kids attended the Bible study. Members took turns reading the Scripture passage aloud. Some of them could read well, but some of the big football players had trouble. When their turn came, instead of their usual response, "Pass," these big football players read. They might stumble, but they were willing to try, and no one made fun of them. After all, if anyone laughed at the football players' reading, they'd be laughing at me too.

God's not looking for ability, but availability.

The teens and I had a relationship of mutual respect. We grew together as we studied the Bible. This is where I learned God's not looking for ability, but *availability.* If we can risk stepping out of our comfort zone into the Spirit zone, God will provide the ability when we need it. He'll use our weaknesses to make others strong.

These kids did what kids do: they grew up. My own teens were soon out of high school, and I lost the strong connections there. *What can I do to get onto the campus again?* I wondered.

My wondering shaped into a new idea: I would go to college and become a teacher – not just any teacher, but a special education teacher. I wanted to help kids with dyslexia and other learning problems. I wanted to help kids like me.

I pondered this idea for some time. No one in my family had gone to college, and I didn't know how to go about it. But when I went to the University of Arkansas to help my stepdaughter enroll, I learned about Pell grants.

I wanted to start my studies during the summer, but my dyslexia still scared me. *Can I handle college work?* I decided to take a political science course to see if I could do it. I knew it included lots of dates and names that would stretch my abilities and highlight my disability.

I passed with a B. Throughout this time, God continued to grow my desire to reach teens. *I have to get a formal education,* I thought. And my desire grew to learn more about my disability so I could override and overcome it as often as possible.

In the fall of 1986, I enrolled in the University of Arkansas as a full-time student. In the meantime, I began testing to confirm my dyslexia. The forty-two points between my score on the achievement test (spelling, letter recognition, and reading) and my IQ score (standard deviation was fifteen points) made for a clear diagnosis.

Now I had official permission to use taped textbooks. My son taught me how to use a variable-speed recorder, and I listened to my textbooks on the twenty-five-mile drive home from college, continuing while I cooked dinner. I'd listen to the same section again later, looking at the book to unscramble any words I needed. Both during college and afterward, I received invitations to speak to college special education classes because I had figured out how to manage my disability so well.

During my second year, I won an award from the American Association of University Women. I hadn't applied for it, so someone else must have put my name forward. I was president of the honor society, volunteered for Laubach Literacy, and taught reading.

Four years after I began, I graduated with high honors with my bachelor's degree and received my master's degree the same day. My mom, who lived with us, joined us for that special celebration on the University of Arkansas campus. Dad had been dead for about eight years, but when I started across the platform, it all hit. I felt as if he were right there with me. "That's my daughter!" I could hear him saying as I sobbed my way across the stage.

God healed something inside me that day. Dad wouldn't have understood everything I had accomplished, but he would have been thrilled. He was always proud of us kids. What a graduation gift from my heavenly Father!

My teaching career began in an elementary special education class where, for the first few days, the kids played on my sympathies. "Mrs. Goodhart, the other kids are making fun of us at recess!"

I listened to this sad story, but I also watched what my kids could do. *They're responding like victims,* I realized. *They want me to go out to the playground, yell at the other teachers, and discipline the kids who are bullying them. They also think they can behave any way they want.*

Once I woke up to their manipulation, I had some discipline to take care of – not with the bullying kids, but with my own. By the end of the first week, I was ready.

"Sit down and be quiet!" I told my students. One of them had crawled under his desk, and another was drinking glue. "Cut it out, and listen."

That got everyone's attention. "Do you want to be in the special class the rest of your lives? Or do you want to go to the regular classes like the other kids?"

"The regular classes," came the chorus. "But we don't know how!"

"I can tell you how, if you'll stop acting like babies." I kept up my no-nonsense approach. "You've got to learn at least a little bit of the things you don't do well." I heard a few grumbles, so I added, "Look, I have learning disabilities too, and I know exactly what you can and can't do. You can't fool me, because I'm one of you!"

They couldn't believe it. I went to the principal's office and told her what was happening. These kids had much more potential than they were showing. With the exception of a few, I knew they could all transfer to regular classes soon.

Once I explained what I was doing, the principal agreed. She did have one concern, though. "You realize you're talking yourself out of a job."

"I don't care. I want what's best for the kids."

The principal had another suggestion. The high school was crying out for special education teachers. Before long, I was working half a day at the elementary school and half a day in the high school.

I became aware of a deep spiritual battle in both places. In the elementary school, an obvious division existed between the teachers who were Christians and a group of atheists who seemed to oppose almost everything we did. A group of us met once a week in the school basement after hours to pray for the school, the principal, the teachers, and the students. I remember the day we found the school janitor listening in instead of cleaning. We brought him into our meeting, and he came to know Christ. Hallelujah!

At the high school, it didn't take long for my faith to become a problem. Someone complained after I was seen carrying a Bible. "I thought this was America," I responded. "Can't I carry a Bible at any time?"

In the six years I taught in that district, I was reported at least seven times for such suspicious activities as praying silently over my kids, putting up a "God's in all of us" sign that one of my students had made, and displaying a manger scene. My students' parents knew and approved of everything I did. It was those outside my classroom who wanted to cause problems. The battle became more and more obvious.

God used this opposition to increase my dependence on Him. It took courage beyond my ability to walk into a classroom and teach reading when I couldn't pronounce all the words or straighten out all the letters. At times, I froze. I had graduated with fancy papers and letters after my name, but I kept wondering if someone would take them away.

About that time, I discovered a wonderful invention called the Franklin Speller. It allows you to type in a word the way you think it should be spelled, and a list pops up with spelling options. It also reads the word out loud when you click on it. I used the Speller to help me teach sixth grade reading. But God was teaching me to trust not in technology but in Him.

Every morning on the way to school I put on the armor of God (Ephesians 6:11-18). He was heightening my awareness of the battle to prepare me for the mission field and the attacks I would face there. He was also moving my heart out of the classroom and toward the work He had for me overseas.

My work with the students was important, I had no doubt. But God had many more lives much farther away who needed to be brought out of the dust and into relationship with Him. And I had no idea how soon – or even how – He would move me there.

Out of the Dust: Follow that Bag!
(as told by Fran Turner)

Go Ye Ministries has close connections with area schools. And I always remember that those began with some unusual instructions.

The first year we came to Peru [from Canada], everything was an adventure. We were way out of our comfort zones. One day, we were going out to do ministry, but I was sick and had to stay back. But before they left, I wanted to pray with my small group. God gave me the definite word. "Follow that bag!"

I had no idea what that meant. But as soon as our prayer time ended, I opened my eyes and saw a bag blowing in the opposite *direction of the wind. Talk about being freaked out! God showed other members of the group clues like "children" and "uniforms" and "over a hill."*

I was still feeling sick, so I went back to bed and slept the entire morning. But my team followed the bag and the other clues straight to a school.

On that very first trip, that very first year, my team connected with the teachers. Would you believe on that day, twenty-two teachers and students gave their lives to Christ? My team leader from Canada was also a teacher, and he connected with the people from the school in a special way.

Because of the relationships made that day, the kids from Casa de Paz went to that school the next year. Go Ye didn't have the Generation of Leaders school at that time, so our kids got to go to this school. And God used our "Ask the Lord" – and a blowing bag – to make the connection.

CHAPTER 10

Redemption

The spiritual battle at school seemed small compared to what I faced on the mission field. I got a glimpse when I left to serve the first time in Honduras. Remember the tubs of children's clothing and supplies that almost didn't make it onto the plane (Chapter 1)? That gave me a hint of the work and warfare ahead.

On that same Honduras trip, I had the privilege of serving alongside Gerizim Church's associate pastor. Pastor Oscar took me out to pray at the home of a woman in the final stages of death.

This woman had several daughters who didn't know Christ. Pastor Oscar and I could sense the spiritual warfare going on, but we could also sense the Holy Spirit's power. During our visit, the sense of His presence grew so strong that some of the daughters fell to their knees, weeping in repentance even before we prayed with their mother. Later, we learned that the mother was healed – and all the daughters gave their hearts to Christ. Hallelujah!

I also traveled to the countryside to the orphanage sponsored by Gerizim Church. When American teams came, they cooked and lived apart from the children. But God gave me different instructions. "Whatever they [the Hondurans] give you to eat and drink, do it with them." He also said something else: "When you're sick, don't tell anyone except me." These two specific words from the Lord became a key part of my ministry then and now.

Pastor Roberto Ventura, Gerizim's lead pastor, must have noticed my connection with the nationals. He invited me to go with him high in the mountains where few Americans had ever been. I felt as though Jesus had asked me to come along.

Some villages were too remote to be reached by road, so we hiked in with our supplies and held services by torchlight. Pastor Roberto would say, "Preach now," and God always gave me something to say.

Most of these people couldn't read, but they knew how to worship. I loved sharing God's Word with them as they shared His Spirit with me.

On that same trip, we visited a small café in a home. Pastor Roberto and I sat alone at a table. "Hallelujah!" he said.

"Hallelujah!" I answered. "Praise the Lord!"

"Praise Lord," he responded. "Coca-Cola!"

"Coca-Cola?" I responded, and we both laughed. He had just spoken every bit of English he knew.

Soon, they brought us something called sour corn soup, served in bowls made from half a coconut. Up until then, my stomach was upset, but the soup seemed to settle it.

"Good missionary," Pastor Roberto told Gladys.

"How come?" I asked after she translated.

"Because you ate the soup."

This trip gave my faith a huge boost. I have no doubt that God's power still works as it did when Jesus walked this earth. And He'll do amazing things through us if only we make ourselves available.

Even before my trip to the mountains, though, I was asked to speak at a women's meeting in downtown Tegus.

I'd never preached before, let alone given an altar call. I spent the day before the meeting praying in the Spirit, as Jude 20 tells us, and seeking God. *Lord, use me,* I prayed as I walked back and forth. *I don't know what I'm doing. It has to be you, not me. If you don't show up, then it's not going to happen.*

> *If you don't show up, then it's not going to happen.*

I felt as though God was asking me to share about the sexual abuse in my past. *Surely not, Lord.* The next day, a uniformed driver took me to the hotel by private car with several other women from the group. We prayed in the Spirit the whole way there. High above the hotel in a luxurious banquet room, 125 well-dressed women sat around tables covered in white linen tablecloths. They seated me next to my translator at the head table. After we ate, I would speak.

Praying silently, I began my talk by sharing my testimony. "Tell about the abuse," the Holy Spirit urged.

What? I've never talked about that in public. I've hardly talked about it at all. And with a group of rich women I don't even know? God, are you sure?

He was. "I want you to tell them your story."

I told about the ongoing abuse from Uncle Jim and another uncle who had also touched me inappropriately. "I felt trapped," I told the women. "I knew I must be a bad girl and what happened was my fault."

No whispers, no clinking of glasses – everything seemed to stop as I continued. "My life was filled with unhappiness, blame, and darkness," I said. I explained the joys of life in Christ but didn't stop there. "Even after I came to know Jesus, my life still had an empty place because of what happened to me as a young girl."

I continued. "But one day, after Dean and I married, my Aunt Ruth called. I hadn't heard from her in maybe twenty years, but she and Uncle Jim wanted to come see me."

I looked around the room before adding: "I couldn't believe it. I felt like that trapped little girl from long ago. I started praying in the Spirit until a peace came. And then God spoke: 'I am doing something great, if only you will trust me and have the courage to walk it out.'"

"This couple who never traveled and had never left Ohio before was taking a trip through our area and wanted to see us," I continued. "I was now in my mid-thirties, so Uncle Jim would have been in his sixties. And I was still as scared as that little eight-year-old girl."

"I had told my husband all about the abuse. I knew I needed to forgive my uncle, and Dean understood that too."

The women still seemed caught up in my story, so I kept going. "They called when they got to Prairie Grove. We said we'd come and meet them. Since there was only one pay phone in our town, we knew right where they were.

"We drove into town, parked, and saw them about half a block away. I got out of our car as Jim jumped out of theirs and ran toward me, his face twisted in pain and regret. He pleaded, 'Forgive me! Please forgive me!'"

I paused. "In that moment, God poured out His grace. 'You're forgiven,' I told him. Uncle Jim sighed in relief.

"This decision freed me. The pain that bound me was gone. By then, Aunt Ruth caught up to us. I don't think she ever knew what happened so long ago.

"God never causes something like sexual abuse. We live in a fallen world, and bad things come into our lives. I knew God was good, but I wasn't sure He could love someone like me." The room remained silent.

"I wouldn't go to Uncle Jim, so God brought him to me. As

my faith grew, Jesus became Lord of my life, and I started ministering to others." I looked at the intent expressions. "God used every bit of my past. I know how wonderful healing is because I know what He did for me. And He can do it for you too!"

I didn't know what to do next, so I closed my eyes and began singing in the Spirit. "Ask who else has been hurt like this," the Holy Spirit urged.

Then, "Have them stand up." Half the roomful rose.

I kept following the Spirit. "You women who are still sitting down – if you're a Christian, stand up and hold one of your hurting sisters.

"Now, everyone who has suffered abuse: Picture yourself as that sad, shamed little girl, scared and alone, locked in your secret. Jesus comes and lifts you up, and His love flows down into your hurts. 'You're safe!' He tells you."

Throughout the room, women were standing, weeping, and clinging to each other. "Linger here and let Him hold you," I continued. "Relax. Feel the peace, the healing, the awareness of good. Let everything go that has kept you in bondage – the hurt, shame, secrets, guilt, intimidation, insecurity, violation. You were robbed of the innocence of youth, the smiles of your spirit. Just abide. You and Jesus can return to that time together when you're ready."

As I spoke, I was watching the women's reactions, still praying. "It's okay. Nothing can hurt you. You feel only the overwhelming love of Jesus. Gently, He takes you back to where the abuse happened. It's dark, ugly, and scary, but He carries you, comforting and leading. He'll be your filter as you make the decision to look at that person again.

"You're still the little girl, but sheltered by Jesus, you can now see your abuser in a different way." Again, I took a deep breath. "Now – just like my Uncle Jim – he's no longer scary, but full of regret. Forgiveness comes into your heart and you are free. The shameful secret disappears."

God kept giving me words I never knew I had. "As you turn away, Jesus kneels before you and clothes you in a beautiful white dress. Now you're the little girl He meant you to be, twirling, happy, and free of agony. You walk out of the hurtful past, ready for the future."

By then, every woman in the room was crying joyful, healing tears. I gave time for them to hold each other, pray, and cry some more.

Again, I didn't know what to do, so I closed my eyes and sang in the Spirit once more. When I opened my eyes, the woman right in front of me was crying so hard she was shaking. I reached out to her in compassion but couldn't touch her because of the podium between us. She fell to the floor.

Did I kill her? I rushed around the table, praying she would live and dragging my translator with me. Others helped her stand. The Spirit gave me words, and down she went again.

That night, a miracle happened. God gave me individual words for many of the women there, which brought incredible healing.

I've never seen anything like this. I've read about it in the Bible, but now it's happening! After the meeting ended, all I could do was lie flat out before Him. I had never been under the anointing like that.

I knew my life was changed forever. God was using me – unworthy, know-nothing me. I was filled with gratitude. I didn't know it would happen, but Jesus healed them all. Until then, I had never shared my full story, but He has lovingly used it many times since.

At the age of fifty, I was on my first mission trip, traveling alone. Now I understood the reason for all the warfare: God wanted to use my story of pain to free others. And I knew He had much more to do.

After two months, I went back to my classroom, but I couldn't wait to get back to Honduras. And I couldn't wait to see what else God had in store.

Out of the Dust: Jorge and Margarita
(as told by Isabel)

God loves to work in unexpected ways. Several years ago, an old man named Jorge ("Horhay") started coming to the Marcos 6:15 church. He walked slowly, with tiny steps, but he came to church every Sunday. He had to start early, but he always sat in the front row.

Later, he grew too old and sick to go to church. Pastor Auden was here at that time, and he took some of us to visit Jorge at home. The old man explained that he had given all his sin to Jesus – that he had been saved for three years. "Pastor Auden, I want you to pray for me, because very soon, I'm going up there [pointing to heaven]."

We all prayed, and I noticed tears running down Pastor's face. Later, when I asked him why, he said, "While we were praying, God told me his time would be short."

Jorge's daughter, who lived with him, was helping cook for a Canadian mission team a few days later. She stopped by to check on her dad, and he said, "Daughter, give me a bath, and make me clean."

She needed to get back to the mission team, but she did as her father said. The homes in Las Palmeras have no running water, so she had to get water from a community site, washing him as he sat on a chair beside his bed.

"Father, I must go back and cook for the team," she said as she dried him off.

"Yes, I understand. Thank you for making me clean, my daughter. Gracias. God bless you. I'll see you."

She returned one hour later. He had died sitting right there in his chair. God let both Pastor Auden and Jorge know his time was short. And because of Jesus, Margarita knows she will see him again.

On this earth, he was poor, but he was clean and ready for heaven. God took him out of the dust.

CHAPTER 11

Struck Down

I returned from Honduras a changed woman. Not just because of what God had done there, but because He chose *me* to do it.

For years, my eyes bore the same sad expression I see on some of our children. Everywhere I went, a sense of shame and dirtiness accompanied me. Satan was doing his best to keep me on the sidelines. And that's where I see so many believers today, put out of commission by a past event. Maybe they were abused. Maybe they feel inadequate. For them, fading into the pew is the safest route.

It's a lie. The deceiver uses our own memories to sidetrack us. But I learned to do what all believers must: Focus on my identity in Christ Jesus. Through Him, I can do anything (Philippians 4:13).

We're forgiven. The limits of our abilities no longer bind us. We are Jesus' inheritance with new resources, new talents, and renewed spirits.

Many years ago, God invited me to come out into my spirit, where bodily limitations disappear. Suddenly, I understood: my spirit me is so much bigger than my body me. Our spirit joined to His Holy Spirit opens limitless resources.

God wants us to think outside the mental boundaries we set. We must learn to depend on His abilities in us to accomplish whatever He calls us to do.

When God showed me these truths, I was sitting in our little country house in Arkansas. But the beautiful life Dean and I had built there didn't seem quite as beautiful anymore. The small, store-front church we attended didn't like my mission trips. "All this talk stirs people up too much," the pastor told me. I knew what he meant: Get right (according to the church's idea of good, safe Christianity) or get out.

Our little town had several churches, but few if any believed in being empowered by the Holy Spirit to the point of doing something real, much less speaking in a prayer language. But that wouldn't keep me from serving overseas. I started saving money and collecting supplies for the next summer's work. God wanted me to move beyond my abilities. And He wanted me to do more than sit around waiting for His blessings to fall.

Even before it began, this second trip seemed different. "Sis, what would you think if Mary and I tagged along?" my brother George called to ask.

"Woohoo! I'd love it!" I responded.

Before long, we had a plan. I would minister in Tegus while they served in the orphanage. George could re-roof the buildings while Mary mothered the children.

This trip also brought with it an incredible spiritual battle. One local pastor took me deep into the city to help release people from demonic spirits. As we prayed, God delivered, and Satan fought against us.

The attacks also came because of my message. My original schedule involved ministry to ladies' Bible study groups. But God kept pushing me toward large congregations, where I felt compelled to share the teachings of Promise Keepers.

"Get under God's authority so you can lead your family with

integrity," I told the men."When you do this, just like the jailer in Acts 16, you and your household will be saved."

One Sunday, I had the opportunity to speak at two services in the twenty-five hundred-member Gerizim Church. That afternoon, I would minister in a sister church of a few hundred people. George and Mary joined me for the day. At lunch, I admitted my exhaustion.

"George, I can't do it," I said. "I can't speak this afternoon.

"Of course you can!" he answered, spearing another bite of spicy beef.

The limits of our abilities no longer bind us.

"I have nothing left," I said. "Could you and Mary speak on marriage instead?"

George and Mary aren't preachers, but they live a sermon every day. People often tell Mary, "You two can't be married. He treats you too nice!"

They agreed to speak after a little more persuasion. The people accepted their beautiful portrait of marriage as a God-ordained teaching.

My schedule the next day included a lunchtime visit with an influential woman. "Lunch, but no preaching," I told the coordinators. "I'm exhausted."

That noon, about forty people – including four or five pastors – filled my hostess's home. When they asked me to open my Bible, God again gave the words. But soon, I felt thirsty. Someone offered me my favorite fruit tea, but I couldn't seem to drink the right way. Still, I kept teaching, and God took over. Holy Spirit power filled the room, and all I could do was proclaim His truth.

Before I knew it, almost three hours had passed, and delicious smells came from the kitchen. My mouth didn't water, but my left eye did. I wiped it and kept preaching.

Finally, the group left, and I wiped my eye again. I hadn't

thought much about what was happening. But Mary hurried over, full of concern. "Avis, you've had a stroke."

"No, I'm okay."

Hands on my shoulders, she pushed me into the bathroom, where I gazed at my face. The left side seemed to have slipped down an inch or two. *What happened*?

"Let's not worry about it," I told Mary as we sat down for our long-delayed lunch.

I soon discovered I couldn't eat the right way either. Food kept falling out of the left side of my mouth, so I held my napkin up to my face and kept eating. *A little spill can't keep me from a good meal.*

Later, I returned to my host home, eager for some sleep. I expected no further problems, but everyone else was concerned. "You have to see a doctor," they insisted. After so many protests, I had to agree, and someone made me an appointment for Tuesday morning.

But I didn't like that plan either. I had an opportunity on Tuesday to speak in a church that ministered to women from the city's red-light district. The pastor said we could broadcast my message to the hundreds of street women outside. I didn't want to miss this open door. So after consultation with the doctor's office, we reached an agreement: When it was time for my appointment, they would send a runner to the church.

Satan interfered again. On our way to the service, a taxi hit our car. Although no one was hurt, we were stuck until the police released us.

We finally reached the church. No street women. No service. We'd missed it all.

We'd also missed the runner. "He came, but we didn't know where you were," the pastor said. "I'll have someone take you down to the office."

I soon had a diagnosis for my facial paralysis: not a stroke, but Bell's palsy. "It usually heals in eight to ten weeks," the doctor explained. I could no longer close my left eye, so he taped it shut and sent me back to the house to rest.

A procession of people came by all night long as I moved in and out of sleep. Those who most impressed me were the big, burly men who had heard my teachings. Kneeling by my bed, they asked God's forgiveness and then prayed for me. My amazement overshadowed my pain. *God's still changing lives. What a privilege to watch Him work!*

We were scheduled to fly home the next day. The doctor had given me some pain pills, and George went to the store for bandages. When he couldn't find eye patches, he cut a sanitary pad in half and taped it over my left eye.

Walking toward the airline gate the next morning, he growled, "It takes real love to walk through an airport with a woman whose eye is covered in Kotex."

"I'd do the same for you anytime," I responded. We landed in Dallas, picked up George's truck, and got a motel room.

Satan continued his attacks. Throughout the night, Mary suffered intense abdominal pain. We made an early-morning trip to the hospital, where doctors performed emergency gallbladder surgery.

The nurses noticed my eye and re-bandaged it. I felt my flesh beginning to swell and realized the Honduran prescription was a steroid. *Why has my body turned against me?* But this enemy was far more powerful than flesh and blood.

Next, I called my husband. "I look a little different than when I left," I warned after telling him about Mary's surgery. "Do you think you could bring the old Cadillac and come pick us up?" Mary didn't feel strong enough to travel home to Nebraska in George's dilapidated pickup.

Dean came, and Mary stayed with us while George went

home to work. She seemed a little better every day, but I got worse and worse.

Satan must still be angry about what God did in Honduras, I thought. Our Lord had delivered people from evil spirits, restored marriages, and healed countless numbers. All the glory went to Him. All I did was show up in His name.

Mary urged me to visit my own doctor. He confirmed the diagnosis, and the school district where I taught hired a substitute. I was sad not to begin the year with my special education students (I had many of the same ones year after year) but felt sure I'd be back soon.

By November, though, I realized something else must be wrong. The Bell's palsy had healed, the swelling disappeared, and the virus that caused the problem had vanished. *So why is the pain so horrible?* I wondered. The neurologist who examined me said some of my nerves had healed the wrong way. This left me with severe facial spasms, eyes that wouldn't water, and unbearable pain.

Another long round of doctor visits began. I missed my students, but I couldn't return to teaching. Not yet.

I visited the school sometime that winter. My changed appearance didn't bother my students, but my crooked smile scared one little girl I didn't know. She ran away, and for months afterward, I went out as little as possible.

I finally wound up at the Mayo Clinic in Minnesota, where I received Botox shots to relax the cramping in the left side of my face. These reduced the pain and improved my appearance, but the nerve damage had its effect. I couldn't pronounce certain words correctly. I had hearing damage in my left ear and reduced sight in my left eye.

Some speech pathologist friends taught me how to speak and gave me exercises to help me close my eye. The shots, which I still get every six months or so, make the pain much more bearable. I still struggle to pronounce words correctly, but with God's help, I manage.

"How could all this happen to you when you were doing the Lord's work?" people often ask. God's Word says it rains on the just and the unjust. And the Bible also says, *And we know that God causes all things to work together for good to those who love God, to those who are called according to His purpose* (Romans 8:28 NASB).

I know God heals. I've experienced healing and I've also had the gift of healing operate through me. But sometimes, He has another plan.

After months of waiting, praying, and seeking medical help, I received news that the school district would release me on disability. This meant two things: for the next fourteen years, I would receive two-thirds of my salary; and I was free to become a full-time missionary.

What Satan meant for harm, God used for good. And there was much more good – and many more trials – left to come.

Out of the Dust: Fran Turner's Story

Healing is still a part of Avis's ministry. I still remember what happened during our church's trip to Pacasmayo in 2009. Pastor Jeff and I split the team to do a feeding. A translator named Paolo went with our group.

I wanted to meet tons of people because we had lots of food to hand out. We were in the Las Palmeras community, and I said, "The next open door I see, I'm going in!"

In one of the adobe block houses, Paolo saw an open door. Of course, he pushed me toward it.

"I don't want to go in!" I said, suddenly afraid. But I knocked

and heard a rude "What do you want?" in Spanish. The door was open, but I saw nothing inside.

Nothing, that is, until Paolo pushed me through the door. There, I found José, a frail older gentleman, lying in bed. I didn't see much more than the bed, a night table, a chair, and a dirt floor. No kitchen. No one else to care for José.

Once he saw my white skin, he grew more polite. He started talking so fast that Paolo couldn't translate. But when José held up a bottle of medication, it didn't take long to figure out that he wanted us to get him some more.

"My fever has lasted many days," he said.

The Holy Spirit came. "I don't have money, and I don't have any medicine, but I'll give you Jesus," I told José. We prayed for his fever to go away, and I saw something leave his body.

When we entered the house, this man could barely sit up in his bed or move. But when the fever left, he bounced on the bed, "Hallelujah! Praise the Lord! Hallelujah!" We couldn't have held him down if we tried.

We left there and went back to the compound without a word. Normally, I'm a bubbly, loud person, but I didn't know how to articulate this. I was in awe. God had done it all, in His way and time.

Even when someone had to push me through the door.

CHAPTER 12

But Not Destroyed

❧

"You're under condemnation, Avis. You need to get out."
Those words came from my new friend Betty. She was hosting our mutual friend, Pastor Roberto Ventura from Honduras. After hearing about my church's negative reaction to my mission trips, she had some advice. "You need to start your own ministry. My husband can help."

What Betty said made sense. I wanted my church's blessing, not opposition. And with my forced exit from teaching, I knew God was leading me to do more mission work. So Betty's husband, a CPA, started helping me incorporate and obtain 501(c)(3) status as a nonprofit.

In order to complete the paperwork, I would have to become an ordained minister. That's another God-story, because He used a pastor I didn't know who served in a church I didn't attend. My evangelist friend, Carol Granderson, belonged to Pastor Layton Reed's church in nearby Oklahoma. After much prayer, I called to ask if he would help me become ordained.

"Why don't you come over, and we'll talk about it?" he said. I drove over that Wednesday, and he asked about my experience in both Bible teaching and missions. We also shared our views on Scripture and theology. But at the end of the afternoon, we still hadn't discussed ordination. Instead, "Why don't you stay for our service tonight?" Pastor Reed asked.

"Okay." *I hadn't planned on it, but if he's suggesting it, why not?*

He came over to me as the service began. "God's told me to ordain you now." Forget licensure, forget setting aside. We both recognized God's work. "After the choir's finished, I'm going to call you up front."

As he laid hands on me and prayed, Pastor Reed spoke some words I still remember:

"I ordain you, Avis Goodhart, with the spirit of unity, Psalm 133:1-3. I see God pouring out the spirit of unity upon you."

But ordination didn't finish the incorporation process. At my attorney's office completing more paperwork, I had to give my new ministry a name. *All I know how to do is go*, I thought. "That's it! We'll call it 'Go Ye Ministries.'"

Within a few months, both ordination and incorporation were complete, and the nonprofit status was on its way. I had a partially paralyzed face, a "disabled" label, and a burning desire to go and tell. Beyond that, I had no idea what God had in mind.

"Lord, I don't know anything," I told Him. "I've been on a couple of missionary trips, but that doesn't qualify me."

"This ministry will be a platform," God said. "With it, you can take others who want to serve." I had come to know many people in other countries who needed help. "As you and the people you bring minister to the nationals, I will minister both to them and to you."

"God, all I know how to do is go," I said again.

I felt Him speak into my spirit as clearly as if He were standing beside me. "Go. I'll show you when you get there."

I had spent most of that school year hiding my twisted face and seeking medical treatment for the problems that caused it.

But there came a day when my doctor said, "You need to get out among people more."

He was thinking *shopping*. I was thinking *mission trip*. It was time to stop focusing on my pain. I had seen God send all kinds of people on mission trips. They weren't Bible experts, but open-hearted, willing-handed people who deeply loved Jesus. And He did amazing things through them. Sometimes the female team members had only one responsibility: holding women as they cried. Love covers a multitude of sins, and sometimes, a compassionate touch was the only thing needed to release pent-up pain. *God can use me no matter what,* I realized.

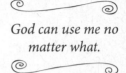

God can use me no matter what.

My Bible teacher friend from Siloam Springs, Carol Granderson, was going to Peru in March, 1997. Her ministry, Power & Light Gospel Outreach, opened international Bible schools and took short-term mission teams overseas. Her students made up most of the group, but I tagged along.

First, we went to Lima, Peru, to work with a church called *Luz Para Las Naciones* (Light for the Nations). We did street evangelism, ministering to the poor. Then Carol asked three of us to split from the team and minister in the city of Pucallpa along the Amazon.

We stayed in the simple home of a pastor. This family had moved from the jungle because of the constant fighting. Leaving everything behind, they walked away with nothing except Jesus and each other. While we stayed there, we held crusade services in a large church. God used me even with my twisted face. The anointing came, and many received salvation and healing.

We then rejoined Carol's team in the high jungle, where people were so responsive to the gospel. In some of our services, we ministered to more than three thousand people. The trip was over all too soon, but not before I made plans to return.

During my time in Lima, I met Maria, a pastor and evangelist. She and the head pastor of Light for the Nations befriended me.

"Can you teach the Bible?" Maria asked one day.

"Sí," I answered

"Can you come back to Peru and teach the Old Testament in our Rhema Bible School?"

I had heard about the Rhema School, a two-year Bible school based in Tulsa, Oklahoma. By now, the Botox shots had improved my appearance, and I could manage the pain. Maybe I couldn't teach school anymore, but I longed to be out there for the Lord. "As long as my husband doesn't mind," I told Maria, "I'll come back in November and teach."

Dean agreed, and I spent the next few months preparing. It seemed almost no time until November arrived, and I was saying good-bye and making the long flight to Peru again. On that trip I taught for two hours, five nights a week. I spent each day preparing the night's lesson. A translator helped make sure my students understood every word.

I battled illness throughout the trip, feeling sick to my stomach while I planned my lessons. But whenever I taught, the anointing came. I still followed God's instructions from my first mission trip: "When you're sick, don't tell anyone. Just tell me, and I'll get you through it."

I figured out later that in the trip's twenty-eight days, I preached or taught twenty-five times. I learned again that God doesn't need our health or ability. Our availability and willingness are all that matter.

Of course, ministry didn't stop on the weekends when we had no Bible school. We held an open-air crusade in Lima and saw many people come to Christ. And on one of the final weekends, we made the 400-mile trek to visit Pastor Jorge's hometown, a small city in the north called Pacasmayo.

I stayed with some local people and preached in a little

church. I also met three women from the poverty-stricken neighborhood of Las Palmeras, built on the dump on the hills above Pacasmayo. Almost the entire community consists of women who moved in from Peru's mountain regions to escape the constant fighting of the drug lords, including the dreaded Communist group, Shining Path. Most of their husbands were involved in these wars, so these brave women gathered their little ones and left.

At first, the women made camp on the beach. Their only possessions were the few things they had brought with them. They stayed there until the government gave each of them a tiny piece of land, about twenty-five by forty feet in size, on top of the dump high above the ocean.

This land belonged to a wealthy family, but no one knew where that family went. For many years, the property had been used only as a dump.

The women did the best they could to construct houses using cardboard, plastic, or bamboo. I saw children sleeping on sheets of corrugated tin, flies covering their faces. One of the mothers admitted in tears that she slipped out at night to prostitute herself in order to earn money for her children. *There but for the grace of God go I.*

I agreed before the weekend ended to help begin a Las Palmeras feeding station. *Someone needs to show them God's love. Why not me?*

As we planned the feeding station, I had no idea God would call me to plant my life there. But I had other work to do first. I was beginning to look and act more and more like a full-time missionary.

After a month, I returned to the United States for Christmas but was back on the missionary road in January 1998. Pastor Jorge and Maria met me in Honduras this time. I wanted to help them learn more about ministry and bless Gerazim Church all at once. I also brought in a team. We stayed only two weeks, working in orphanages, holding a medical clinic, and taking a group of thirteen to Nicaragua. But the two Peruvian pastors stayed an entire month.

One afternoon not long after I returned to Arkansas, I stopped at McDonald's. I happened to overhear a family speaking in Spanish. I had to introduce myself when they kept mentioning Peru.

That began a God-ordained relationship. The husband, a Peruvian, had just graduated from Youth With A Mission's Discipleship Training School. He and his American wife were helping plan a conference called Explosion '98 in Leticia, a free zone between Colombia, Brazil, and Peru. Deep in the jungle, Leticia could only be reached by plane or boat.

My new friends explained the conference details. Planned to reach thousands, it would include workshops for parents, pastors and their wives, youth, youth leaders, and more. "Come join the women's teaching staff," my new friends urged.

Sometime that spring, I started taking five or six mission trips a year, a month or more apiece. Dean finally said, "Please don't stay longer than three weeks," and I did my best to honor his request. Before I knew it, I was on my way to Explosion '98.

My good friend and translator from Honduras, Gladys Montoya, met me in the Bogota airport. We spent the night and flew to Leticia together the next day.

You never know what relationships God will bring you. At that first Explosion event, Gladys and I met Leyla de Poblete from Iquitos, Peru. She already worked with FRANKA, a new, growing organization for battered women. Back then, if a Peruvian woman filed for divorce, the man would get the children. That law kept many women from leaving abusive marriages. And many of these same women were battered in the name of submission.

But Leyla's message was different. The Lord gave her a mission to unify and strengthen women by teaching them His true ways. She came to the Explosion, in fact, to get area pastors' blessing on a women's conference she hoped to hold the next year. When I taught on the unity of women, she almost jumped out of her seat.

There at Explosion '98, a sisterhood was birthed that lasted several years. With Gladys's translation help, Leyla and I organized an intercessory group connecting the women from villages up and down the Amazon with a larger group of women in Iquitos. And God allowed us to lay the groundwork for the women's conference too.

After Explosion '98 ended, Gladys and I left Leticia in a Peruvian air force seaplane. We heard about this unusual taxi service from someone else at the conference. "To get your tickets," our friend explained, "Rent a motor-powered canoe and cross the Amazon. When you reach the village on the other side, ask for the Blue Lagoon Bar, and buy your tickets there."

It sounded like a movie scene. But by then I'd been in Latin America long enough to believe it. And it was all true. "Catch the plane in two days at that sandbar," the man at the Blue Lagoon said, pointing out into the river.

We met the plane as instructed. This was no luxury taxi service but a small seaplane with no interior walls. The pilot handed us life vests that looked and smelled like hundreds had worn them. And he packed people into the plane like sardines. Gladys and I looked at each other, our eyes revealing the same thought: *What have we gotten ourselves into?*

We flew – or I guess you could say bumped – over the mountains to Iquitos, visited some contacts, and then flew back down to Lima.

Next, it was time to return to the new feeding station. Gladys and I made the twelve-hour bus ride and spent three weeks ministering in Pacasmayo before flying back to Arkansas. To help both of us, Pastor Roberto paid for Gladys's trip. She would have a season of refreshment in the States, and I would have her help with the organizational work and newsletters for the new women's prayer ministry.

Once again, God made a way where there seemed to be no way. And that was something I would have to remember in the days to come.

Out of the Dust: Fred Miller's Story

Avis is right. Our first trip to Peru was something else. My brother George and I, along with our wives, flew into Lima and took a bus to Pacasmayo. We stayed with one of Avis's friends and helped with some open-air revivals. Then George and I took the bus back to Lima and flew to the Amazon to put in a well.

We stayed in a grass hut for a week, and it was two weeks before Avis and our wives caught up to us. We felt like we had gone back in time.

When we finally got the gasoline water pump hooked up, we tried it out. It threw the water from the Amazon forty feet in the air. The people had never seen anything like it, and the kids ran around, waiting for us to squirt them. We all had a great time.

But other things were happening while we were helping villages get water. We brought lots of medicine along with three nurses and some local doctors. The medical team held a clinic and checked for all sorts of problems. And we were all building relationships, working to make connections to plant a church.

Peg and I went ahead of the team on our next trip there and boarded the ship in Iquitos an hour or so before they did. We saw the crew use a narrow ramp to load a huge black Brahma bull, which kept jumping off into the water.

That should have been a clue that the boat would be a real experience. It held about two hundred fifty people and what seemed like thousands of chickens running around loose on the roof. It had open-air sides, a pipe running down the middle, and another down each side. You tied your hammock to those pipes and slept up against your buddies. Many people just slept on the floor. And on the metal roof above tramped not only those noisy chickens but monkeys, pigs, goats, and a herd of cows.

But the great thing about the crowding was all the opportunities to talk about the Lord. We had a projector, and I figured out how to hook into the boat's power source. So we showed the JESUS film and other Christian movies as we traveled down the Amazon. At the end, we always did an altar call, and many people got saved.

As we look back on it, it's all been an adventure – a highlight of our lives.

CHAPTER 13

Hurricane!

Over the years, I've faced both physical and spiritual storms. But Hurricane Mitch was one I almost didn't survive.

Gladys spent her summer as we'd planned, helping me get all my mission work organized. She got word in late October that her father was ill. She had to return to Honduras right away.

That turned out to be God's providence, because just after she reached her family, Hurricane Mitch hit. Overwhelming though it was, she would never have wanted to be away from them during this time. The massive amounts of rain caused everything from flooding to mud slides to earthquakes.

Listening to the news, I couldn't imagine the devastation in this country I'd come to love. Water lines broke, bridges blew out, sewage flowed onto the streets, and in many places, communication was destroyed.

The mayor of Tegus and other city officials went up in a helicopter right after the hurricane hit to survey the damage. When it crashed, everyone inside was killed. The city had no leadership left.

Once again, God gave me the word: "Go." The members

of my Tuesday morning prayer group all agreed: I must obey. They also agreed to help in any way they could.

As usual, I wanted to take more than myself to the country. *Everyone's talking about Hurricane Mitch. Surely they'll donate food and supplies.*

One of my prayer group friends contacted Tyson Foods, who agreed to send a brand-new, fifty-three-foot semi-truck along with a driver who would help me get to Brownwood, Texas. There, I would load whatever I collected on a ship bound for Honduras.

On Wednesday, Tyson parked the semi in the nearby town of Lincoln, and I spread the word. I peered inside the truck bed the next evening to find one lonely flat of supplies clear down at the far end. "God, you've got to give me more than this."

I'd gone all over our town trying to drum up support. But when I saw the near-empty trailer, Satan ripped me up one side and down the other. "You have a whole semi, and nothing to fill it with. You won't be able to help anyone!"

He and I fought it out through the entire night. By the next morning, a radio station had somehow heard about my plans. They sent a reporter out to the lot where the semi waited. "Even if you get it filled, how do you plan to take it into Honduras?" he asked me. "They won't let it cross the border!"

"Oh, yes, they will," I told the reporter. "I'm going with it!"

"You're kidding!"

"No, I'm not. I'll go – and it'll get in," I promised. "But for now, we need stuff: clean clothes, rolled up and ready to go. Think about what it's like to be in a flood and have all your clothes stripped off you – to have nothing." I knew those words would connect with the radio audience, since many had survived floods themselves.

But God wouldn't let me stop with clothes. "These people need food, too: good food, and lots of it. And if you give me a can, give me a can opener, too, because everything's gone. We need meat and peanut butter. We need water and bleach." I paused again to emphasize my point. "Don't give me your junk. These people need help!"

No sooner did I finish the interview than supplies began to pour in. But I knew God wanted more. I went to the Farmers & Merchants Bank and asked to speak with an officer.

"We don't have any food, Mrs. Goodhart."

"No, but you have money, and that buys food."

I left with a check.

Next, I went to the phone company with a similar speech. Then I stopped by the local grocery store. They did have food, and gave us $500 worth right away.

Two of my prayer partners knew God wanted them to give. Mr. Dean, not a wealthy man, told his wife: "Write a check for $1000. We'll cash it, go to the canning company, and buy as many flats of food as we can."

Every time I went back to the semi, I found people dropping off supplies. Friday morning, my friend Lorene stopped by. A former bookkeeper for the University of Arkansas, she liked to keep things in order. The chaos she saw in the semi horrified her.

"Avis! They've got stuff all over the place," she said. "Would you like me to organize it?"

Would I? "Sure!" Lorene hoisted herself onto the truck bed and went to work. If clothes were on hangers, she folded and put them into boxes. If four different pallets held green beans, she moved them all onto one. Nothing went into the truck without her sorting and labeling. Her work let us fit many more supplies into the semi and freed me to keep asking for more.

On Saturday, November 7 (the day after my birthday), Tyson sent the truck driver, who turned out to be a pastor's wife, one more confirmation that God was preparing our way. We chugged out of Lincoln at noon with more than forty-five thousand pounds of supplies – from diapers to blue jeans, from cases of water to canned goods. "Praise God!" I kept saying. "Hallelujah!"

Early the next afternoon, we reached the Brownsville dock. A forklift driver made quick work of the trailer's contents, and my sister in Christ took off on another run.

The next part of my adventure began when the owner of the shrimp boat spotted me on the huge dock, where he had already started sorting out the supplies. "Whoa, what are you doing here?" he asked.

"I'm with the stuff," I told him. "I'm going to Honduras too!"

He made it clear he didn't want me on the dock. And he definitely didn't want me on his shrimp boat.

"I'm not leaving," I said. *Time for another prayer walk.*

"God, you called me. Fixing this situation is up to you." I climbed down in front of the dock and marched back and forth. Singing one of my favorite hymns, I grew louder with each pass: "The cross before me, the world behind me! No turning back, no turning back!"

It didn't take long before He used my singing to help me see what He already knew: I was going to Honduras. He was in charge, and He would get me there.

Before long, Captain Kent from the shrimp boat appeared. "Come home with me," he urged. "Spend the night with my family."

It was getting dark, so I did as he said. We had a great evening of dinner and conversation.

When we returned the next morning, things were looking up. Captain Kent, his two crew members, and I hand-packed all my supplies over the next three days. They all had to go on the deck because the hold (the area underneath the boat) was full. We moved the supplies off one pallet and hoisted them onto the barge. There we put them onto another pallet and, once it was full, sealed it using huge rolls of plastic wrap.

Those few days taught me two things: a boat must have permission to leave the country, and everyone on board needs a reason to be there. In order to leave the U.S. legally, I had to go to the port office and register as the cook.

As it turned out, my new friend Captain Kent was also the port captain, in charge of bringing ships in from the ocean to the dock. He hadn't been out to sea in four years.

By now, the boat owner's wife and I were fast friends. We finished up in the late afternoon our last day in port. "Let's go get something to eat," she said. The owner, his wife, and I went out for a delicious Mexican meal.

After our hard work, I'm sure I overate, a small choice with big consequences. The crew was putting the last-minute maps and charts on board. The sky looked gray, but all we saw on the ocean were gentle waves.

Once we left the harbor, though, everything changed. Our peaceful boat became a roller coaster. The crew members went into yellow-slickered action, tying stabilizers in place and doing everything possible to keep the boat safe.

As a first-time sailor, I sat, taking it all in. *It's getting rough out here.* A wave washed onto the deck right then, splashing over me and out the other side. And as fast as the wave had come, a stream of vomit shot out of my mouth. I looked around, wanting to apologize for the mess. Another splash of sea water washed it all away before I could say a word.

My stomach emptied once again. I looked around only to realize no one cared. They were too busy trying to keep the boat upright. A wave roared across the deck for the second time and swept away my mess.

Everything was rocking and rolling. All I could do was collapse in the doorway and try to breathe. One of the men dragged me farther into the cabin next to a pallet of boxes. "Just stay here," he urged.

"Euuuuuhh," I moaned in response.

I stayed in the same spot for three days. I was lying next to the bathroom, but I was so sick I didn't realize it until the third day. Then, Captain Kent came over and yelled down at me, "Mrs. Goodhart! Mrs. Goodhart! You stink!"

He shoved me into the bathroom along with a pair of big, baggy pants and a sweatshirt. I sat on the floor and let the stream of the shower flow over me as the boat pitched and rolled. Finally, I managed to shut off the water and pull on the clean clothes.

What I couldn't do was open the wooden bathroom door. Captain Kent eventually heard me struggling and rescued me again. Yanking open the door, he tossed me into the bottom bunk a few feet away. He hung a sheet from the bunk above me as a crude curtain.

I stayed there another two days, hardly moving. Every so often, the cook urged me to drink some hot milk: "It'll be good for your stomach."

I don't know if I drank any milk or not, but I did wrestle a bottle of Coke from my backpack and take an occasional sip. But on the fourth day, I opened my eyes to calm instead of chaos. Captain Kent carried me out onto the deck and into a peaceful scene.

Everywhere I looked, I saw the beauty of the Lord, including creatures I'd never seen: flying fish. These stunning, silvery beauties skimmed a few feet above the water, traveling as far as thirty yards in one movement. A few landed on the deck. "Lord, I'm so happy to be here," I prayed aloud. "It's beautiful! Hallelujah! Praise God!"

By this time the crew was laughing at me, or maybe with me. "Thank you for your goodness, Lord," I continued. "Hallelujah!"

Whether they liked it or not, I was having my own little praise party there on the deck.

That night, we sailed into more rough waters, following the storm as it made its way across Honduras. The squall had destroyed most of our navigation instruments, including the depth- and distance-finders.

Night fell, and the water pushed in. The men dropped the anchors, but my stomach was already rolling. "God, can you just get me out of here?" I prayed. But another thought came: *If I die down here, nobody will know where I am. What about Dean? What about my kids?*

But then I remembered: *God's in charge.* The crew stayed up almost all night to keep us safe. And the next morning, we reached a small island, Guanaja.

One word described it: *barren.* Trees without leaves. Houses without roofs or walls. Everything was blown everywhere.

> But then I remembered: *God's in charge.*

As soon as we lowered the anchor, people rushed the boat. I tried to go call my friend Gladys, waiting for me in Tegus, but I couldn't navigate the crowd. People started throwing items off the deck, but their supplies were all in the hold. Captain Kent stopped the riot, barking orders and pushing back the crowd.

The Port Authority soon showed up. That quieted one situation and presented another. Because we'd entered their port, the officials wanted fees. Captain Kent had an answer: "We brought all this stuff to your people. Don't ask us for money too!"

He and the officials somehow reached an agreement. We offloaded the supplies from the hold, pulled up the anchors, and left Guanaja as soon as we could. We had no ministry base there, and for all we knew, conditions in Tegus were just as bad or worse.

Finally, we were on our way, the forty-five thousand pounds

of supplies on the deck mostly intact. As night fell, I started noticing tiny lights like fireflies in the water. At first, I saw only flickers down by the bow, but they kept growing. "Captain Kent," I called. "Why do I see fire in the water?"

"That's sea fire, or phosphorescence," he said. "Some of the sea creatures leave phosphorous in the water. The first boat that goes through afterwards releases it, and it glows."

I didn't care too much about the science, but I knew who made the sea and its creatures. "Hallelujah! Praise God!" I repeated as I gazed at the starry beauty flashing from the sea.

I praised God throughout the eighteen-hour trip. Tegus isn't a port city, so we landed in Puerto Cortes instead.

Once again, the sight was nothing short of unbelievable. Huge vessels made our shrimp boat look like a toy. Germany brought in massive water tankers because the hurricane had destroyed so many water lines. Mexico docked a gigantic hospital ship with a helicopter flying from it to a camp city in downtown Tegus where a medical team performed triage. Dead bodies lay everywhere.

Once we reached the harbor, the Port Authority refused to admit us. I told them about my letters, supply list, and anything I could think of. "I'm meeting Gladys Montoya. Her husband is the major of police in Tegus," I added.

Nothing seemed to work, so I kept praying as Captain Kent negotiated and six men lined up to keep us on the boat. A small pickup soon arrived. A short, official-looking man got out and marched toward us.

As I watched, he stopped. "Sister Avis!" he exclaimed. Nothing could hold me back. I leaped over the railing and gave him a hug. Not only was he in charge of all the officials there, but his wife was Maria, the administrator at Gerizim Church. She visited my home with Pastor Roberto when he came to the U.S. Gladys had told them I was coming, but the three-day delay confused everyone.

"Come with me," said my new friend. He made phone calls, filled out paperwork, and got the ship cleared to unload with two big trucks to transport the supplies. We hired men from the dock to offload everything. It was nearly dark before they finished, and here came Gladys at last.

She had waited and waited three days earlier, but when I didn't show up, she went home. We were so happy to see each other, and now I had a partner in praise. She and I went in one truck and Maria's husband in another. The hurricane had destroyed many bridges and roads on the 115-mile drive to Tegus.

At sunrise, we reached our destination. Because of all the post-storm looting, the city was under martial law. When Gladys showed her I.D. to the soldiers who stopped us, they changed from rough and tough to "Yes, ma'am!" We were the first relief workers to get through to that whole area of town. Although more than nine thousand people lost their lives in this tragedy, not one person from Gerizim Church was killed. We thanked God for His protection and knew He would use us to minister hope.

By daylight, all we could see was destruction. The slick roads were covered in mud. Almost every treetop had furniture or other household objects lodged in it, and any houses that remained had suffered horrific damage. Hurricane Mitch's terrible power had stripped most people's clothes from their bodies. They covered themselves with blankets or anything they could find.

I remained in Honduras for two more weeks. We've had some terrible disasters in our country, but the Hondurans had no insurance, no savings, no anything. Yet they still managed to smile.

Gladys and I went out to the refugee camps set up in the

state schools, where the scenes were equally unbelievable. People were trying to cook in old paint cans or discarded pieces of tin. The hurricane filled the outhouses with water and mud, but everyone needed them. Gladys and I dumped bleach in each facility to help prevent disease, working like crazy to help in any way we could.

On one of the first afternoons, I saw a big Coca-Cola truck heading up the mountain. "Look at them, taking advantage of people who have nothing left," I told Gladys, sure the company was making money through disaster relief.

Later that day, one of the area men told us about the visit from the truck. "They handed out bottles of water and soda," he said. "No one had to pay."

There amid the tragic scene, I had to stop and repent. My words reflected my poor attitude. I judged the company without knowing the truth. Later on, God would remind me of this incident whenever I was tempted to question someone's motives. There are always things we don't know.

I stayed in the refugee camps as long as I could to distribute supplies. Once the airport re-opened, I flew back to Arkansas. I would be off on another mission trip to another country in only a few more weeks. Missions was becoming more than a summer activity. It was becoming my life.

Later that year, I returned to Honduras, and I couldn't understand why I received such special treatment. Many churches invited me to speak, and people offered anything I needed.

When I started speaking at the first church, the people interrupted. "This is good, but we want to hear about the boat."

The boat? I didn't come on a boat.

"Tell us about when you came on the shrimp boat to help our people after Hurricane Mitch," they insisted. *That was months ago. How do they even know about my crazy trip?* But I told the story anyway.

The woman who drove me back to my hotel that day had tears in her eyes. "You shame me," she said. "You cared more for my people than I did. You *did* more for my people than I did. But no more!"

It was then I knew God had taken the story of one unlikely missionary and used it to wake up His people. More and more, I sensed His calling to serve overseas full-time. I knew I would do it.

And it wouldn't take another storm to wake me up.

Tia's Story

Mom's mission work wasn't much of a family issue at first. My brother and I had lives of our own, and our stepdad always supported her in anything she did.

I started to get a clue about how serious Mom was about missions when she started doing trips down the Amazon. But the first time her mission work caused a real problem was during Hurricane Mitch.

Long ago, I decided she had a few blank spots when it came to safety. She'd go into a part of town where anyone I knew would be on guard. But Mom would just march right in as if she had no idea of the danger.

I really thought she was naive. It's taken years for me to realize this is part of the way God made my mother. He used it to prepare her for what she's doing now.

The trip after Hurricane Mitch brought a new level of concern. Because I'd served in the military and still had connections there, I always had a Plan B. If something happened, we could find a way to locate my mother. But this time, I wasn't sure it would work.

From my years in the navy, I knew what a fishing boat was.

I tried to explain it to her ahead of time, hoping she'd realize it wasn't the best idea.

But before I knew it, she left. When we didn't hear from her for days, I called the Port Authority in Honduras. They weren't functioning, so I tried the Red Cross. "We're not in there yet," they told me. "It's not safe."

Great. I used my military connections to contact the air force base in Tegus. "We're not flying out. It's not safe."

That's when it hit me: My mom was on a fishing boat in the ending throes of this hurricane. And I might never see her again.

I kept praying about the situation and for her. At first, I was really angry with Mom. We couldn't find her, and everybody was concerned. But I finally got to the point where I realized that more than anything, this was her choice. This was what she wanted to do.

I had a mental process to go through similar to those with family members in the military. Your loved one is making a choice to put themselves in harm's way, and you can either support them or not.

I had to go through that process with, of all people, my mother – my school-teaching, church-going, casserole-making mother. This was the first time I realized she may have chosen to put herself in a situation where she could actually die.

There came a point when I had to say, "This isn't CNN, this is my mother, and she may not come home." When she finally called after about ten days, I'd already released my anger. I was overjoyed.

Even today, I let Mom have the enthusiasm God gives her about things. I have to keep giving her to Him and not live in anger or fear.

CHAPTER 14

Mountains of Blessing

⟨ ⟩

In July of 1999, I traveled to Leticia, Colombia, to teach at Explosion '99. This was the fourth annual conference held in this city for pastors and church leaders along the Amazon in Colombia, Brazil, and Peru. I felt excited to have a small part in God's great work.

The conference lasted for five days, and I taught several of the women's sessions. These Explosions were a huge operation. A separate team of people was working this year to train youth and children's workers along with another team in charge of the five hundred children who attended. A team of young adults did street and jungle ministry, and a medical team performed surgery for those in need.

We held a citywide crusade at night in a huge amphitheater with five to six thousand in attendance. By the end of the week, God was bringing eight to nine thousand people each night. It became almost impossible to get near the amphitheater.

Hundreds of people came to the Lord through this wonderful week. Everywhere I looked, I saw people either ministering or being ministered to. God met physical, spiritual, and emotional needs through the Explosion.

One of my extra blessings was sharing a room with two Wycliffe missionaries who had given their lives to Bible translation. One showed me the leathered soles of her feet. "That's from running through the jungle," she said. She was living the life of a true missionary, becoming like the people she served.

My new friend's feet may have been tough, but her heart was soft to the things of God. The guerilla fighting had driven her family from their jungle community in Lomalinda, but not from their life's work. In fact, she brought the most recently translated portions of Scripture to the conference to give to some tribal men who met her there. Her family had to get out, but she still wanted to get the gospel in.

Another conference blessing was reconnecting with my friend Leyla de Poblete from Iquitos, Peru. I team-taught with Leyla, the head of the women's intercessory prayer group we began in July of 1998. Many of the women we taught belonged to that same prayer group and had come great distances by canoe.

I felt blessed to work with this precious woman of God. Since she didn't need an interpreter, she could teach twice as much material as I could. We saw great spiritual growth in our students, along with a deep hunger to know more about Jesus. We could only imagine the hardships and dangers they faced every day, but the new friendships strengthened the body of Christ throughout the Amazon region.

Our main conference speaker was Dr. Ruth Ruibal, an American who has lived most of her adult life in Cali, Colombia. Not long after graduating with her Master's in Public Health from Columbia University in New York, she moved to Cali, where she met and later married Julio Ruibal, "the apostle of the Andes." Together, they founded a church in La Paz, Bolivia and another, Ekklesia Colombian Christian Center, in Cali.

Julio Ruibal worked hard to promote unity among Christian leaders and pastors in Cali. But in December, 1995, he gave his life as a martyr, killed by a man closely connected to some of the drug cartel's hit men. This man was furious about the church's location on a property adjacent to his. After killing her husband, he put Ruth, her two young daughters, and the leadership of their church on a hit list. Over the next five years, he threatened their lives again and again.

But Ruth knew the call of her life was to Cali, so she and her daughters remained there, and He rose up in her like a lion. During the years to come, Ruth would travel to thirty-five countries speaking,

> *You intended it to harm me, but God intended it for good.*

teaching, and preaching her husband's message on the unity of the church. The apostle of the Andes had not died in vain. As Genesis 50:20 says, *You intended it to harm me, but God intended it for good to accomplish what is now being done, the saving of many lives.*

God used her husband's death to open the ears of many nations to the message of unity. They saw the power of God in this widow who wouldn't run.

But the violence continued. During the week of the conference, the Colombian government and the U.S. military were fighting in the jungles against the drug lords. Yet the conference atmosphere was all peace and joy. Although we knew about the ongoing violence, we never saw it. *And the peace of God, which transcends all understanding, will guard your hearts and your minds in Christ Jesus* (Philippians 4:7). He was faithful as always.

And Ruth spoke powerfully despite the violence around us. An American helicopter went down, and several military personnel were killed, along with more than a hundred Colombian civilians lost during the riots. When the American Embassy ordered U.S. citizens out of the country, we had to end a day early and head to Bogota.

Most people left the country right away, but I couldn't change my flight. I made it to Bogota but had to wait to return to the United States. A young preacher from Texas chose to remain behind with me.

"You don't speak Spanish, ma'am. I can't leave you here alone," he said. We stayed in a YWAM mission base. On Sunday morning, we tried to attend an English-speaking church. When we arrived, it was empty except for the pastor. Invading guerrillas were threatening to hold Americans for ransom. "Get off the streets," officials said.

During all this chaos, one of the doctors we knew from the conference drove us to his daughter's birthday party. High in an apartment building in downtown Bogota, we enjoyed the family fiesta while the tension escalated on the streets below.

The next morning, the YWAM staff took my Texan friend and me to the airport, and we finally headed home to the United States.

I was soon back in Honduras for an entire month. The main purpose of this trip was to open a feeding station in Tegus. My earlier contacts birthed a wonderful partnership that helped with the many details.

The trip also provided opportunities to preach, teach, and provide clothing and Bibles for two separate Indian groups in two different areas of Honduras. I still marvel at the way God gives people a hunger for Him. The nationals would walk for hours to reach the meetings, staying as long as anyone would preach or teach. It all left me more in awe of God and His work.

I received an invitation while in Honduras to visit nearby Nicaragua. I went with a group of Honduran pastors and church leaders for a three-day Clamoring (season of prayer). Watching these men and women love and serve built my faith. How could I not support their work to spread the gospel throughout Latin America?

God also gave me more opportunities to preach at Gerizim Church and its clinic. He was truly preparing the way for Go Ye Ministries, both back at home and in the hearts of the Honduran people.

Meanwhile, back at the feeding station, we had more work to do. God opened the doors for me to preach to a more affluent group of Hondurans. One businesswoman gave us one hundred plastic cups, bowls, and plates. Others reached into their pockets, purses, and bank accounts to meet the ongoing needs.

Few people in Honduras have the financial means to help, but Gerizim Church sent some of its resources our way. They gave us the building to house the feeding station and committed to its daily operation. Our team was temporary, but Gerizim would be here long-term, and these children needed long-term help.

The feeding station, a one-room, one-slab wooden building with a concrete floor, sat halfway up a mountain. Its windows had wooden shutters but no glass. The only way to reach it by car was to drive higher up the mountain, circle around, and then descend on a slippery, muddy lane. When we began, the women from Gerizim were cooking on campfires each Saturday, trying to feed a hundred children. Most of these women knew poverty well. They lived in homes made out of anything they could find, with dirt floors and no running water.

Each week, these twelve women scraped together every bit of food they had to feed the children. Only the Bible study teacher had a book, but the children sat and listened with great interest. They also sang together and answered questions about the Bible. God was working in many small hearts because these women cared enough to give out of their need.

Go Ye Ministries soon received enough donations to purchase a commercial stove and refrigerator. I loved seeing the women's faces when the truck chugged down the hill and the driver opened its doors to reveal the sparkling appliances.

Go Ye was also able to provide enough money to give the children a healthy meal each Saturday from September until February. We didn't have enough funds to feed the children every day, and many had nothing. By God's grace, we grew enough not only to feed these children more often but to open several other feeding stations. These eventually settled into a routine, and soon we were feeding eight hundred children three times a week.

During that same trip, we also built a brick room onto the back of the first one-room feeding station on the mountain. This new room would house an area woman who would stay each night to guard the stove and refrigerator as well as the food itself.

The entire community shared our excitement and wanted to help. The small children carried one brick at a time down the mountain. Older children and women lugged bucket after bucket of water uphill for mixing mortar. Everyone helped shovel sand.

To this mountain community, the feeding station brought not only food, but hope. The people joined us in thanking God, naming the station *Montaña de la Bendición,* "Mountain of Blessing."

Of course, God didn't limit His blessings to the people of Honduras. He had more work to do in blessing the nations. One unlikely missionary was taking other equally unlikely people to serve in Latin America. Together, we would serve out of our weakness to pour forth His strength.

Out of the Dust: Manuela Castaneda Garcia's Story

Avis has touched many lives through the years. I first met her in the home where she was leading a Bible study and helping women learn to make crafts. I remember her as a young, pretty woman, always happy. I loved spending time with her and would come whenever I could.

After a while, I started seeing that the difference in her life came because of God. "How can I invite Him into my life?" I asked. Because of Avis, I accepted the Lord. She gave me a Bible, and little by little, my life changed. I started listening to God more and more.

My family has come to the Marcos 16:15 church from the time it first began. My children and my husband all received Christ there, and my daughter sang for the church services.

I felt sad because I didn't have a Christian family growing up. But then I met the people from Canada and the United States who came to help our church and community, and I realized that God works in all of us. Now, I am a part of a family of believers, and I'm so happy.

God has given me a special ministry of prayer. I pray much for the church and for Avis. When my Christian brothers and sisters are sick, I pray for them, and it's as if God puts me right there in the hospital with them. If they're having surgery, I feel like I'm having surgery myself. Sometimes my family doesn't understand that part of my ministry, but the important thing is that God knows. And I will serve Him no matter what.

CHAPTER 15

Go Anyway

*O*ver the next couple of years, I made almost more mission trips than I could count. God gave me the idea sometime in the year 2000 of taking a used van to my friends at Gerizim Church. Vehicles cost much less back home than in Honduras, so I decided to buy one at auction and drive it down.

Of course, I had no intention of driving an empty vehicle all that way. I would fill it with plenty of clothes and other supplies to help the still-struggling nationals. Generous friends donated once again, and we soon had the van crammed so full I couldn't use the passenger mirror.

I was all set to go when my brother Bob called from Phoenix. He didn't like the idea of me driving by myself, so he and his wife offered to follow me in their car. We met in San Antonio and spent the night.

The real journey began early the next morning. By this time, I knew the enemy often used government officials in his attempt to thwart God's plans. I made a careful list of everything we carried. I called ahead to the Mexican government, offering to fax the list, but they said to bring it along. *Easy enough*, I thought.

Not exactly.

We reached Brownsville about noon and went across the border to Matamoros. Here, we had our first battle. The border agents didn't like our papers; they didn't like the supplies we were carrying; and most of all, they didn't like us.

"You can only go a few miles into Mexico, and then you'll have to come back," they said. They wouldn't even consider letting us take the van all the way to Guatemala (between Mexico and Honduras). We waited at the border for three days, returning every morning to try again.

A border agent stepped out of her booth the morning of the third day and pulled me aside. "I'll help you," she whispered. She couldn't change the rules, but she knew a priest who ministered to people living on the town dump. "He can use your stuff," she said.

After more discussion, we took her advice. We had to get the van to Honduras. After the agent came off duty, she led us to her simple home. We unloaded all the clothes and supplies before spending one more night at the border.

I felt sick inside. My friends in Honduras needed everything I was carrying, but I had no way to get it there. *Lord, let this priest be the real deal. Use these supplies to bless these people even more than you would have used them in Honduras.*

The next day, we drove through Mexico, spending the night in a beautiful little town with cobblestone streets. We awoke refreshed and ready to cross into Guatemala. But at the border, the officials wanted to spray insecticide under both vehicles. We had paid for the same treatment at the U.S.-Mexico border, and now, more officials demanded more money to redo it. After a vehicle impoundment and a desperate call to my translator friend Gladys, we finally crossed the border – but not without another fee.

Our final border crossing, from Guatemala into Honduras, brought its own share of problems. When you take a vehicle into a country, the government expects you to bring it back out. Our intention to leave the van caused another snarl of paperwork along with a third fumigation request. Our planned three-day trip had now stretched to ten.

That wasn't the first time I faced unexpected obstacles as God moved me forward in missions, and of course, it wasn't the last. Not long after the van adventure, I took a team of thirteen into Honduras. We brought shoeboxes filled with toys and other children's items along with medical supplies.

This was back before the days of severe baggage restrictions, so we planned for everyone to bring along two large tubs filled with items we wanted to deliver. I called ahead, and the airline okayed the containers as long as they stayed within the weight limit. The team agreed to confine their personal luggage to one carry-on apiece. We ended up with twenty-five bins of shoe-boxes and medical supplies and one shared bin filled with the team's tennis shoes.

When we got to the airport, the trouble began. An airline counter employee refused to check us in.

"But the children at the feeding station need these supplies," we told him. "What can we do?"

We turned our prayers into action. One at a time, the team members opened their carry-ons and began putting on every piece of clothing over the clothes they already wore. They then transferred the items from the tubs into their now-empty carry-ons.

"That's enough!" the man at the counter finally said. He checked in the remaining tubs and watched our overdressed team members march onto the plane like robots, their limbs stiff with extra clothes. They didn't care how they looked. They just wanted the shoeboxes to reach the kids.

That trip ended up as a combination of medical and dental ministry, shoebox delivery, and drama ministry. While the health professionals worked together, the rest of the team evangelized, and we touched many lives. Once again, we partnered with Gerizim Church, who provided translators and other help.

I helped coordinate another medical mission trip, this time to Iquitos, Peru. Our work began by holding clinics in three remote villages along the Amazon. The heat and humidity overwhelmed us, but the joy of being Christ's hands and feet gave us strength. After the medical professionals left, four of us flew over the mountains to hold a weeklong revival in the beach town of Pacasmayo, where I had served a few years earlier. We traveled to Lima next for some speaking engagements.

We held one of the large-group meetings at a huge Sheraton hotel, where God did something amazing. One of the speakers and her husband owned three television stations, so we wound up on TBN for all of South America. Only God could have granted such favor.

I experienced more favor later that summer when I spoke at a huge women's conference in Manaus, Brazil. But I also saw the obstacles the enemy sent my way. I was all set to fly out from Miami – or so I thought.

"Where's your visa?" the ticket agent asked.

"Visa? Won't I get it when I get to Brazil?"

No one, not even the travel agent, had told me to apply for a visa ahead of time. My suitcases went to Brazil without me. The airline paid for three days in a hotel as I waited for the Brazilian embassy to grant my visa request. It took a phone call to an ex-senator from Arkansas to straighten everything out.

I arrived at the conference only moments before I spoke. Since my luggage was still locked up in customs, I wore the same clothes as when I left home four days earlier. "I'm glad the stage is high above you, so you don't have to smell me," I told the women. Several of them came up as soon as I finished speaking and offered to lend me some clothes.

I soon saw the reason for all the problems: God's great plans. Our main speakers were Ana Mendez of Mexico and Ronnie Chavez of Argentina. One evening, Ana and her translator; my translator, Leyla; and I were all being driven to the stadium where we would speak. The two translators were chatting away when Ana spoke quietly, almost to herself, "Tonight, God is going to give me Portuguese."

"How do you know?" I asked.

"Well, he's given me German, French, Italian, and English when I needed them."

"Do you get to keep them?" I asked, dumbfounded.

"I am speaking to you in English, am I not?" Ana smiled.

"Yes, you are. Very good English." When we reached our destination, I waited to see this living miracle. More than nine thousand people filled the stadium as Ana walked back and forth in front of the platform, praying.

An usher escorted the rest of us to our seats down front. When the first speaker finished and the host introduced Ana, she and her translator went to the center of the stage. "Listen closely," I told Leyla. "I want to know what she says and what language she says it in."

Ana's translator stood a few feet from the podium while Ana began another march, on stage this time. She stopped in front of the podium and told the audience, "God is giving me Portuguese right now." She then proceeded to preach for two hours in perfect Portuguese. She stopped every once in a while, turned to her translator, and said, "How do you pronounce [a certain word] in Portuguese?" After she got the answer, she went right back to teaching and preaching.

On the way back to the hotel, I asked, "Ana, how does that happen?"

"Not with the mind, but through the spirit," she answered.

"You can't use your mind." I didn't understand, but I did trust the same God.

I returned home in August for some minor surgery. "I've got to heal fast," I told the doctor. "I'm taking a medical team into the Amazon soon."

Dean took great care of me while I recovered. We enjoyed a rare time of rest until the sad day in September when a friend called, urging us: "Turn on the TV."

We stood frozen in our living room as images of the Twin Towers filled the screen. "Dear God, help those people, and help our country," we prayed. That day, our nation and our travel changed forever.

A week or so later, still in shock, I had to decide about our upcoming trip to Peru. Our team included thirteen members from the United States, three Korean doctors and nurses, and several Peruvian pastors and assistants. Some of the Peruvians would travel great distances by bus. Could I still ask the Americans to go?

God called me to go, so He'll take care of me.

We were scheduled to leave in early October, only three weeks after the tragic events of 9/11. The threat to Americans traveling outside the country was high, and we had no idea if the government would allow us to fly.

One at a time, I called each team member. Everyone gave the same answer: "God called me to go, so He'll take care of me."

All was well with our souls. God was preparing us once again for the great work ahead.

Out of the Dust:
Auden Lujan's Story

I first met Avis in Prairie Grove, Arkansas, through a mutual friend. Later, I realized God was setting me up to work with her.

If you've ever met Avis, you know she talks to you right away about whatever's on her heart. "I just started a Bible study with a group of women, but I don't know what I'm doing. I need somebody who can speak the language," she confessed.

When she asked about my education, I told her I had studied discipleship. "Well, you can come and teach a discipleship course," she said, as if it were already settled.

"I'll pray about it," I told her, more of a standard response than a promise.

But before long, I came to Pacasmayo and taught a month-long discipleship course. Avis was ready as soon as we finished. "Would you be interested in coming here full-time?"

I laughed. "Avis, you know I'm a pastor. I have a life!"

I've always liked missions, but I wasn't ready to serve in Peru. Still, "Nothing is impossible with God," I said.

I was still praying about her request at Thanksgiving. I told God, "You know I want to do what you want, but I don't want to make a mistake, either. I don't want to leave the people here. But if you want me to go, I'm available. Since I don't seem to get it, please give me a sign."

I asked God for a specific date, December 16. "If it rains that day, I'll go." In my country, the rainy season is May through September. It doesn't rain in December, so I wasn't making it easy on Him. But on December 16, it started sprinkling. I told God, "That's just a little bit of rain, and it doesn't count. I won't know you want me to go unless it really rains!"

The next thing I knew, it was pouring. And it kept pouring all night long. I woke the next day and said, "Well, God, you win."

Over the next few months, I got everything in order. I came to Pacasmayo in September 2005 to pastor the Marcos 16:15 church.

Two or three days after I arrived, I met a mission volunteer named Wendy. Travel problems had postponed her visit, or we wouldn't have met. We were married just over a year later and have lived in Peru ever since.

Avis is a very persistent person – you might even call her stubborn. Even when everything is against her, she still keeps going in obedience to God. That encouraged me. And sometimes when things were hard, I would think, "Well, if Avis is doing it, then I can do it too."

To me, Avis's message is that whatever deficiencies you have, they're no excuse to say, "I'm not going to do what God has called me to do." So many people are so qualified but waste time wanting everything to be perfect before they do something for the kingdom of God. It's sad to see, because it's really not you but God who does everything anyway.

Just like Avis always says, "It's gotta be God."

CHAPTER 16

Legacy

~~~

*O*ur month-long mission trip couldn't have been more min-
istry-filled. We did day-long medical campaigns in three
different villages along the Amazon. As soon as the lookout in
each village spotted us, he would beat his drum to let everyone
know we'd arrived.

The houses consisted of slabs of wood cut from large trees to
make a wide platform on stilts. People traveled between them
by canoe. Each home had open-air sides and a low, thatched
roof to provide shelter from the daily downpour.

In a corner of each house was a boxed-in area filled with
sand where the family built a fire for cooking. The center part
of the home was often closed off with curtains or bamboo to
provide a bathroom of sorts. The toilet consisted of a hole cut
in the wood. The waste went into the river where, a few feet
away, you might see people using a bucket to get drinking
water, washing clothes, or bathing. I'm not easily shocked, but
these unsanitary conditions amazed me. They also inspired
my brother Fred to drill wells for some of the Amazon villages.

One day, our team went downriver from San Juan, the
small village where we set up camp. When we tried to return,

the boat motor stalled, so we left later than planned. Night was falling, and traveling upriver was difficult because we had no real lights. Fred sat on the bow, watching for drifting logs and other debris. He could only turn on his flashlight every so often because its batteries were low.

We finally made it back to camp, but not to rest. The wife of the San Juan pastor was in labor with their eighth child, and things weren't going well. Dr. Kim, the Korean doctor who headed our medical team, wanted to transport her to a clinic farther downriver than we had traveled earlier. Fred rigged up some lights, and he, the doctor, and the laboring woman headed out in our water ambulance. Early the next day, a healthy baby girl came into the world. Her unusual name matched her unusual birth story: Avis.

We held services every night as we traveled up and down the river. But like every ministry, this one carried a cost. There on the Amazon, mosquitoes are both huge and plentiful. I preached at night in a long-sleeved shirt, ankle-length skirt, and oceans of bug spray, with only my face exposed. Mosquitoes kept trying to fly into my mouth whenever I spoke.

We brought gifts of medicine, tools, shoes, clothes, and Bibles. But most important of all was the gift of Jesus, and many of the people accepted Him. This fruit of our labor made even the giant mosquitoes seem small.

Now it was time to fly to Pacasmayo once more. On this trip, we held an open-air crusade and worked with a small church called *Jesus Es Mi Pastor* (Jesus Is My Shepherd).

God deepened the burden on my heart for the people – mostly women and children – who had fled the fighting of the drug lords and ended up in Las Palmeras. I knew I had to do more than visit. I had to do more than preach, "God will help you, just be patient," and return to the land of plenty. Scripture says, *If anyone has material possessions and sees a brother or sister in need but has no pity on them, how can the love of God be in that person? Dear children, let us not love with words or speech but with actions and in truth* (1 John 3:17-18). We should use discernment about how and where we give, but our compassion must move us to action.

We had already opened a feeding station, but God was giving me a vision for a larger ministry. I wanted to help these women build better lives for their families. At the time, I pictured my brothers helping me build a small home. I'd fix a big pot of soup there, enough to feed the women and children who would gather for Bible study and other lessons. I'd have some mats where the street children could sleep, and I'd clean them up and help them get to school every day.

My dream was small but powerful. Before we left, my brother Fred and I started looking for land. I didn't picture myself staying in Peru long-term, but I knew I would need a mission base.

I had to go home first. I could hardly wait to share with my husband my new burden for this place and these people. Dean was leaning up against a wall in the Fayetteville airport waiting for me as always. But this time, he didn't look so good.

"You've lost weight," I commented. "Are you sick?"

"I've been watching what I eat. My back's bothering me a little, that's all."

He stayed home sick on a Sunday morning two weeks later. When I returned from church, I found him on the floor. Together, we got him back into bed, but he was in terrible pain. Against his wishes, I called 9-1-1, and the hospital admitted him later that day.

After a day of testing, a young doctor delivered the bad news: "It's cancer. And it's metastasized."

Dean and I both knew that without God's intervention, he didn't have long on this earth. So he decided to come home under hospice care and spend his remaining days with family.

Our children and grandchildren came often, and I was always at his side. If I left the room, he wondered where I was. Those last months were a healing time for both of us, and God walked with us each step of the way.

"Are you afraid of dying?" I asked one day as he sat in his wheelchair looking out our front window.

"No," he answered. "I just don't want to leave you and the kids."

Dean also spent time planning what I should do after he was gone. "God's sending you overseas full-time, Avis," he said with confidence. "And I want to make sure you're safe when you come home."

He advised me to get rid of the chain saw (he knew if I had it, I'd try to use it), move our son Mark and his family in, and buy a mobile home to use when I needed a break from the mission field. Weak as he was, Dean still did his best to take care of me. How I loved that man!

His gospel group partners came to see him more than once, and we had an old-fashioned singing right there in the house. Sometimes he sang along. But soon, he was too weak to do more than smile.

During these few months, Dean realized for the first time how much people loved him. Early in 2002, our community held a pie supper at the VFW hall to raise money for some of his medical expenses. He was in so much pain that no one expected him to attend, but once he heard about the event, he wanted to go anyway. My son and stepson, Mark and Glen, picked him up, wheelchair and all, and put him in our van.

When we arrived at the hall, the boys brought him in with his IV and other tubes hanging everywhere. We could only stare at the crowd of two hundred who packed the place.

As his sons rolled Dean to the back of the crowded room, people rose in a standing ovation. Not long after we arrived, I heard one of the pies auctioned off for what I thought was sixty dollars. *That's a lot of money for a pie.* Within a few minutes, I realized it went not for sixty, but for *six hundred* dollars. God was providing yet again.

As the evening wound down, someone put a giant red-and-white chicken bucket stuffed with donations onto Dean's blanketed lap. Later, when we took time to count it, we couldn't believe it. Our friends and neighbors had given more than $10,000. And after more gifts arrived over the next few weeks, we had more than $13,000 from our loving community. "I didn't know they cared," Dean said, still in shock.

All our kids were home on February 6 in the late afternoon when I leaned over Dean's bed. He looked around slowly at the loving circle. Then he looked at me, smiled, and took his last breath.

His funeral was one of the largest I've ever attended. It seemed the whole Prairie Grove community was there. When I walked in, I heard his taped voice singing, "One day, I want to stroll over heaven with you." I smiled through my tears as I heard my sweetheart's voice declaring his love for his Savior. *He's not hurting anymore,* I realized. *And I bet he's singing right now.*

I still feel sometimes as though I've lost my anchor. Dean was that for me. He held our grown kids, finances, and home together while I ran all over the place. And he kept track of everything, including me.

> *One day, I want to stroll over heaven with you.*

I set everything else aside during his final months to focus on him. But just as he told me, God was preparing the way for me to serve overseas full-time. He took care of our finances first. Thanks to Dean's wise money management, we had no house payment. But while he was ill, the bills mounted, and the funeral cost more than his burial policy covered. I started calling around to figure out what we owed. With our small savings and the huge gift from the pie supper, I was able to pay off his doctors along with the imaging clinic. But that left the biggie: the hospital.

I made the phone call and reached the accounting department after a few transfers. I explained who I was and that I wanted to begin paying my huge bill. Something incredible happened next. "You owe nothing, Mrs. Goodhart. You're free and clear."

That news still flabbergasts me. It was a turning point, one of those times where you know God is sending you in a particular direction. I realized that being debt-free was a beautiful gift, but back then, I had no way to know just how beautiful.

When I think back, I realize I would never have gone to the mission field with unpaid debt. I would have gotten a job, started a business, or done something else to pay my bills. But that would have kept me home, and the Lord knew that. So He made a way for me to leave with a clear conscience and without any debt.

God showed me again that if I would step out in obedience, He would take care of the details. I would need to remember that lesson in the months and years to come.

Out of the Dust: The Shoebox Lady

Of course, Dean wasn't the only one who invested in Go Ye Ministries. In our early years, almost every mission trip included a shoebox distribution. At first, we asked people to pack them with toys, soap, toothpaste, socks, and other items for children. But because of a few people who gave inappropriate or soiled items, we soon learned to check each box.

Lorene Vickery (the pastor's wife who packed the semi full of items for victims of Hurricane Mitch) became our shoebox coordinator. At first, she went through all the donated shoeboxes to check and repack them as needed. Later, she decided we should ask for financial donations so she could buy and pack the items herself.

Every box contained a new pair of underwear, socks, an outfit, two toys, and toiletries. One year, a woman designed a coloring book that shared the gospel for children. Go Ye mass-produced it and put one into every shoebox we packed.

As she did with the semi, Lorene put the space in the shoeboxes to good use. She didn't send empty baby bottles, for example, but filled them with socks and other small necessities. Every item in every box had a purpose, and with each shoebox came a typed inventory of its contents. People were generous with their donations, and Lorene never wasted a penny.

Go Ye had lots of help delivering the shoeboxes to the children of Honduras and later, Peru. My brother Fred, who lives in northern Florida, would often help us drive a load of shoeboxes from Arkansas to Miami. We had a contact there who bought and shipped refrigerators to Honduras. He offered to ship the shoeboxes at no cost if we helped pack them in and around his refrigerators, so that's what we did.

The packing and unpacking was back-breaking, but we shipped thousands of boxes and blessed thousands of children. Their first shoebox brought many of them their first doll or toy car.

In Prairie Grove, Lorene was known as the "shoebox lady." She never saw any of the children who received our boxes, but she helped change many lives. When she meets those children in heaven one day, I believe they'll know her and how she gave of her time and energy to bless them.

CHAPTER 17

Casa de Paz

⟨✢⟩

God also prepared the way for the next work He had planned
for me in Peru. And He used two of my brothers to do it.

While I was still caring for Dean, Fred and George returned
to Pacasmayo to keep our appointment with the mayor. They
found an available plot of land right there on the dump at the
edge of Las Palmeras, but they needed the city's permission
to buy it.

The mayor and his brother were both engineers, and Fred
is a builder. After they secured the land, my brother drew a
potential church building in the dirt. "We're buying it," Fred
called to tell me. I understood what he said, but I was so focused
on Dean and his needs that the words seemed surreal. I didn't
ask questions. I just kept caring for my husband.

God was using Fred to take my vision to a much higher
level. Instead of a small, simple building where I could care for
only a few people, he planned a large, beautiful church with
a big, modern kitchen and room for ministry to women and
children too.

Before he returned home, Fred took measurements for the
plan he drew in the dirt. Back in Florida, he drew up those plans

and sent them to the mayor, who tweaked them to match the Peruvian building code specs. My vision was moving forward even before I could return to Peru.

By now, Dean had passed away, and I was working to get my life in order. I moved myself and Go Ye Ministries into an eighteen-foot camp trailer, and my son and his family moved into the home Dean and I built. Over the next couple of years, friends and family helped me build a cute two-bedroom house on three acres cut from our land.

Dean died in February of 2002, and that July, I returned to traveling back and forth between Peru and the United States. Only now I was building in both places.

I took another team to Peru in January of 2003 and continued my preparations for long-term ministry. I wanted to meet with the mayor and get a better understanding of the plans he and my brother had made. Fred went along to make sure everything was set up the right way.

The three of us had a great meeting, and the mayor even allowed us to pray for him. After we went over the plans, he looked at me and asked, "When will you begin building?"

I hesitated, knowing the Go Ye account contained only about $2,000. Fred and I bought our plane tickets with our own money, a practice we continue to this day. But my loving, generous brother whispered in my ear, "Go ahead and tell him we'll start now. I'll give you the first $10,000." Go Ye Ministries-Peru was about to open for business.

The whole team participated in a ribbon-cutting ceremony. One of the men on the mission team had a trumpet and another, a shofar. We danced, shouted, sang, blew the horns, and praised God. We made so much noise that all the neighbors came out to see what was happening.

It only took a moment for God to whisper, "Tell them about me." I grabbed my translator and shared a simple, to-the-point gospel presentation. Right there in the dust of the dump community, thirty people gave their hearts to Christ. Using their broken Spanish, the team excitedly took down their names and rough ideas of where they lived.

The team and I flew back over the mountains to Iquitos almost right away for a time of planned ministry before they flew back to the United States. I remained there to teach at a women's conference for four days. Instead of returning to the United States as I had planned, though, I returned to Pacasmayo. I wanted to be there when the building began in earnest, but it was a good thing I couldn't see all the obstacles ahead.

We have become Christians, and we know Christians are supposed to pray. That's why we decided to have this meeting.

The first real construction began at the end of February 2003. My assistant and I were pouring water into deep holes for the church foundation when another woman came by and asked, "Are you going to the meeting?"

"What meeting?"

"A meeting at Isabel's house. All the people who got saved the other day will be there!"

"Let's go!" I said.

I grabbed my Bible and hurried to Isabel's tiny home. Women and children filled the room.

"We have become Christians, and we know Christians are supposed to pray," Isabel explained. "That's why we decided to have this meeting."

The people had only one Bible between them all, but they asked me to teach them more about Jesus. I couldn't say no, but I couldn't leave them with only one Bible either. I made the twelve-hour bus trip to Lima and bought cases of Spanish Bibles and study booklets.

I gave a Bible to everyone who attended the meeting the following Saturday. That was the beginning of our Las Palmeras

Bible study, which became the congregation for the brand-new church. But when I handed out the Bibles and booklets, I had some instructions. "If you don't read these and keep coming to our Bible study, I'll take them away again," I warned. I gave out more than eighty Bibles during the first few weeks alone.

Before long, I combined the Bible study with craft-making. The last time I was in the States, I had prayed about teaching the women to make something they could sell. "God, what can they do to bring in sustainable income, something that won't cost too much?" I asked as I drove to a speaking engagement. There on my dashboard sat a nylon net scrubby used for washing dishes, crocheted for me by a friend.

I took my Father's hint. When I returned to Peru, I brought bolts of nylon net and several dozen crochet needles. After Bible study and prayer, I taught the women how to make the scrubbies. "These will take the good name of Las Palmeras to people in the United States," I said. "It will also be a way for you to bring in money and remind you of how important you are."

I sent the women home after the second week with everything they needed to make more scrubbies. I bought the first samples from those who completed enough to sell. One of the women who came to Christ on the dedication day was first in line to sell her wares. I heard her whisper to herself as I paid for the small handful, "I can buy bread."

God was confirming the work of our hands. And taking time to lead the Bible study and teach the women a skill were both part of His plan.

The whole time we were building the church, we had seventy women and about two hundred children attending the Bible study each week. I kept busy teaching while going back and forth to Lima getting permits and filing all the paperwork to register as a Peruvian nonprofit. We joined various organizations that pertained to churches, nonprofits, and orphanages, and had meetings with attorney after attorney. Only by God's grace was I able to navigate this maze and become registered in Peru.

I also spent time on the paperwork related to constructing the church. The building itself was moving forward, but anything that required a permit, an inspection, or any other government work seemed to take five times as long as it did back home. Fred flew in to help oversee the project whenever he could.

Construction projects in Peru, like almost everything else, are done in a completely different way than in the United States. When Peruvians make a concrete roof, they use three cement mixers. Men climb up and down homemade ladders, dumping buckets of cement onto boards held up by long, slender poles. They keep the poles up for three or four weeks until the concrete dries.

The tradition is that whenever a roof is poured, the building's owner provides dinner for all the workers. I asked the women of our church to cook beans, rice, and meat out in our courtyard. Before the dinner, I once again took the opportunity to share a simple gospel message and pray. We knew we were putting up much more than a building. We were establishing a ministry, and we wanted it to have the firm foundation of faith and obedience to our Lord.

Yet every time we went down the hill to Pacasmayo, we couldn't help but notice the dozens of children begging in the street. If you sat in an open-air restaurant, they came up to ask for your leftovers or beg for money. Downtown, some of them slept in the trees because they weren't allowed to sleep on the streets. But if they were caught bothering the tourists, the police would pick them up and take them away. The town's reputation as a haven for surfers mattered more to the officials than caring for the children.

I met a young teenager named Percy one day who lived on

the streets. Instead of giving him money, I took him out for a meal. "Do you want to eat tomorrow?" I asked him.

"Si, señora," he answered.

I showed him how to pick up the trash at our construction site, and he cleaned it every day. After I bought him a new pair of tennis shoes, his grandfather paid me a visit. "Are you a Christian?" he asked.

"I believe in the Jesus of the Bible," I told him.

"That's good. Will you take my grandson, please?"

"But the orphanage isn't done," I explained. "We have to finish the church first."

Tears welled in the old man's eyes. And that's how Percy became our first unofficial orphan. At times, he still visited his grandpa.

Before long, I was keeping four boys, all young teenagers. They were street kids, and none of them had a place to sleep. Like Percy, they worked with us at the construction site during the day and slept inside the church building at night. But eventually, the government agency that oversaw adoption wouldn't let us keep any children until all our paperwork was legal and complete. We worked to match the boys with families.

I still see Percy sometimes when I'm out and about in town. He's all grown up and drives a *moto* (motorcycle taxi).

As I prepared to return to the States again, our church had begun to take shape. A vision and a plan drawn in the dust had already become a way out. And I counted myself blessed to join God in His work.

Out of the Dust:
Georgina ("Gina") Carrera Grados's Story

I've worked for Casa de Paz for five years. I was a mom (in charge of one of the orphan family groups, or "houses") for three years, and I've been the orphanage director for two and a half years. I am here to help the children, and I love it.

The hardest thing about working here is helping the new kids adjust. When new children come to us, we must work to earn their trust. It is a responsibility, too, because we are under MIMDES (Ministry for Women and Social Development, the government agency that oversees orphanages). If we don't do a good job, the judge can shut us down. We have to be careful with all our paperwork and make sure we do everything the right way.

It can be hard to communicate [with English speakers] *at times, but we get through it. The children are the most rewarding and challenging part of working here. They all come with different attitudes, but when they come here, they all have to change their behavior. We can't prevent their problems, but we can try to help them. The older they are, the harder it is to help them overcome the past.*

When I first came to work here, I worked all day and at night too. We only had a day and a half off every week. It was very difficult.

The most difficult thing for me is when the kids lie or show other behavioral problems. I pray every day and ask God to give me lots of patience.

I would love to see the orphanage have more money so we could make it a better place for the kids. That's why I'm here: to help the children.

CHAPTER 18

Generation of Leaders

W hen I look back over our ministry in Pacasmayo, I can't help but see God's faithfulness. As I write this, we've just finished our seventh year in the Generation of Leaders school next to the Marcos 16:15 church. We began with just six grades, and every year we've added the next. The Peruvian school year begins in March and finishes in mid-December. Our students have won many awards over the years in areas such as chess, marching, science, and sports.

My original vision had nothing to do with a school or even a church and orphanage, of course, but God grew the vision as He grew the ministry. We saw a need, planned to meet it, and watched Him take us far beyond what we could ask or think.

Our orphanage had its official beginning in April 2005. In 2004 we added onto the eastern side of the Marcos 16:15 church in a long wing where we would house the children. We gave it the name *Casa de Paz* (House of Peace) because that's what we wanted to give the children God brought us: peace.

Once we had official state approval, we had no shortage of children. Many of them came to us through the court system. And just as in the United States, many of them were not true orphans. Instead, the parents lost custody because of drug or alcohol abuse, physical abuse, or other problems.

This time of growth was birthed and bathed in prayer. I asked God to bring us the people who belonged and keep out those who didn't. Another prayer that has meant a great deal to me is, "Lord, change me. Even though the grapes dry up, I will praise you."

The longer I live, the more I find myself in a lifestyle of praise. So often I hear people say things like, "I don't know where God wants me" or "I don't know what He wants me to do." But all we have to do is to be willing. He's big enough to move us where He wants.

All we have to do is to be willing. God is big enough to move us where He wants.

Our vision for Go Ye Ministries grew with the need. I'd intended to be hands-on with all the orphanage kids, but before long, the mountain of paperwork and bureaucracy overwhelmed me. I ended up doing more administrative work than I ever dreamed. Because I didn't know exactly how to do it myself, I couldn't tell anyone else how to do it either. And to this day, I often feel like I'm trying to catch up.

Of course the language barrier didn't help move things along. I thought I would learn it by moving to Peru and living among all the Spanish-speakers. But a dyslexic mind doesn't work that way. Even after all these years in Central and South America, I know enough Spanish to get along, and that's all. Sometimes my secretaries have spoken English, and sometimes they haven't. Sometimes I've had translators when I've spoken with government officials, and sometimes I haven't. But God remains faithful. Whether I'm preaching, counseling a child, leading a women's Bible study, or making plans to open a new part of our ministry, somehow, the message always gets through. All glory to Him!

Just as He did years ago in Arkansas, God brought people

alongside me to help with the work of the ministry. Of course I had willing church members, but most of them were brand-new Christians with limited financial resources. None of our money goes as far anymore.

For example, when we began building the church, the exchange rate was 3.47 soles to one American dollar. Today, it's only about 2.58. That means I need more money to do the same thing in a time when most North Americans have less. But God keeps providing. He's never early, but He always comes through.

Go Ye Ministries opened a school to meet the needs of our orphanage kids, who were having lots of trouble with their education. The district that contains the Las Palmeras community is a poor one. The public school is so dilapidated, in fact, that even the office doesn't have computers. And Peru has a law that all its public school teachers are government employees, which means they can't get fired. If they have a doctor's appointment, for example, they just tell the teacher next door and leave. You can walk into a school and find kids running around everywhere.

Casa de Paz couldn't afford to have our kids running wild. Like most kids from rough backgrounds, they needed structure. They needed discipline.

They needed us to open a school.

Our children's need soon became my fervent prayer. I didn't see myself going back into education, but for the sake of our children, something had to change.

I met an older man and his wife, both teachers, one day in the downtown marketplace. After a long conversation, they came to visit Casa de Paz and fell in love with two of our girls. While waiting for permission to adopt them, they started tutoring all our kids. That made a big difference at homework time.

The couple never did get final adoption approval for the girls, but they did get Alex, a curly-haired two-year-old with a smile that would melt your heart. In spite of their ages, this couple wanted him. All the paperwork went through in only a few months, and he was theirs. I saw the little family in the marketplace just the other day, and Alex, now in second grade, seemed healthy and as happy as ever.

Our friends gained a son, but the Casa kids lost their tutors. And the public school still wasn't working out for us. We needed a school that would understand orphans' unique needs and problems. We had twelve-year-olds who had never attended school and fourteen-year-olds who had already given birth. Once again, God prepared the way.

One of our strongest supporters was a Missouri businessman named Al Lockhart. He and I were discussing the problem with the schools when he suddenly said, "Avis, you need to start a school of your own."

"You've got to be kidding. I don't need one more thing to do. I can barely keep up right now!"

"But your counterpart in Moldova [a country in Eastern Europe where there was an orphanage] has a School of Tomorrow going, and it's working out great," he said. "The rich people in town all send their kids to the school, and it's supporting their orphanage. Over the long term, I think a school here would do the same thing."

I gulped. *I want a school, sure, but I don't think I can do this. But Christ in me can do anything.* My theme song, as usual, was "One Day at a Time."

These factors all flowed into our decision. Pastor Auden and Wendy were married by this time, and she was in the midst of a difficult pregnancy. That meant she would soon have to resign as orphanage director.

Wendy had gone to the School of Tomorrow in Lima the year before for a week-long training program. Right after that, we decided to wait another year to open our school. But now we began to file the mountain of paperwork needed. We had several generous backers who were helping us stay afloat during this time.

"Draw up a list of everything you need to start the school," Al told me in his most businesslike voice. "Computers, projectors, desks – don't try to cut it down."

I gulped again. The School of Tomorrow had some specific requirements, and we had nothing except some willing volunteers and a little money in the bank. But we also had Jesus, and He changes everything.

I needed $90,000 to begin the school year – a large amount of money in any culture, but an incredible challenge for a small ministry in South America. And that didn't even include the building. How many millions would it cost?

My brother Fred soon found out about the school. He has to be building something all the time, so he started figuring. He came back to me with the numbers. "For $16,000, I can do it."

"Do what?"

"Build the school. For $16,000, I can divide up that area [a place set aside for housing mothers and babies at the orphanage], put in windows and doors, build playground equipment, and get the electricity going." At the time, we had about $30,000 in the bank because I had just sold my house in Prairie Grove and turned over the money to Go Ye.

"Good," Al told me when I reported back to him. "I have a sponsor who'll back the school. Get started."

I kept on top of the paperwork – or as on top of it as I could in Peru. Fred started building, and we all kept praying. Our projected opening was March 2008. We were running all over getting things ready, spending our own money to build while we waited on more from the sponsor.

Until Al called again. "The sponsor's out," he said flatly.

"What? You've got to be kidding!"

"No. A big fire burned almost everything he had. He's got to put anything extra into rebuilding his business – not into our school in Peru."

Sponsor or no sponsor, we were too far in to back out. I was interviewing teachers, we were meeting with parents, some orphanage employees had left – all I remember is how crazy it was. And in the middle of all that, the government organization that supervises our orphanage, MIMDES, told us we had to start paying our employees almost double what they were making.

We didn't have the money to run the orphanage this new way, and we sure didn't have the money to start Generation of Leaders. But somehow, thanks to some generous givers and the providence of God, we managed to open the school on time.

Since then, we've lived month to month. Sometimes we have money to pay our employees, and sometimes we don't. Sometimes we receive big gifts, and sometimes the funds trickle in. But we've always managed to stay open, and we've experienced the kind of success only God can explain. Generation of Leaders is now known as the best school in Pacasmayo, and just as in Moldova, some of the wealthiest families in Pacasmayo send their children to us.

For the first four years, I served as the school's director (principal). After that, God showed me it was time to give the school to the Peruvians working there. As an owner-operated school, they don't have to operate under the strict pay scale the government required of Go Ye. But they use our building, and we still provide volunteers to teach English and other classes when possible. In exchange, they agreed to let up to fifty of our children attend there free each year.

Sometimes I think we get into a rut of thinking we must have everything figured out before we can step out in faith. But that's not faith. I don't think everyone should quit work and take off for the mission field, but I do think God wants more people who are willing – willing to open themselves up to what He wants. He may not show them a blueprint for the rest of their lives. It may be just one faith-step at a time.

That's what He's doing in me, and that's what He can do in everyone who's willing to trust Him. I didn't come to Peru thinking I would open a church, an orphanage, or a school. In fact, if God had shown me all that up front, I might have turned around and gone home. But now, when I look at all the lives that have been touched and changed, I can do nothing but praise Him. He knew what needed to happen. And He's the one bringing people out of the dust.

Out of the Dust: Georges Calderon Amayna

This is my fourth year to work in the Generation of Leaders school. I'm the assistant principal and also a teacher in the primary school.

I came here the second year after the school was founded, and right away I saw it was a special place. I saw the Christian faith of the people and the way they take care of the orphans at Casa de Paz. I've felt all along that the strength of this institution is its faith in God.

This school has influenced this community for the better, especially because of teaching English. Without that, it's hard for the students to continue with their education.

I think the school has also been a positive influence because of the exchange of social roles. We have students who have money, and then we have the students from Casa de Paz who don't. We made a rule that all the kids here would exchange with each other. We have the same rules for everyone, and we treat them all the same way. Sometimes the parents cause problems, but we have many students with humble hearts, especially some whose families have money. Many of them are willing to befriend the kids from Casa de Paz.

I believe it's a good thing, a very good thing, for them all. And as far as the Peruvians owning the school, few North Americans make this step, but I think it's a great idea.

When I first came here, I was shy. I was ready to teach, but this was my first opportunity. I've learned so much during my time here. I don't have children, but now I work with them in my own church, and I realize that someday, I would like to be a father. But the greatest blessing of teaching here is that I have grown in my faith and I know God better.

CHAPTER 19

Oh, Canada

⟨◦———————◦⟩

Through the years, Go Ye Ministries has been blessed to connect with a number of churches and individuals who have given their time to serve God here in Peru. But the children at Casa de Paz, the staff at Generation of Leaders school, and the people of the Marcos 16:15 church all know one church from one country that stands apart from the rest. Alongside the Stars and Stripes of the United States of America and La Enseña Nacional (The National Ensign) of Peru displayed in our sanctuary, a third flag tells the story. Proudly flying with the others is The Maple Leaf of Canada.

"When's Canada coming back?" our Casa kids often ask. And so do the people in Las Palmeras. They mean the loving people of a Canadian church that has sent multiple mission teams here. You've already read several stories from those trips. But how did a small church in Drayton, Ontario become partners with a small ministry in Peru? Only God could have made this connection. And only He could have done it so well.

Back in 2005, Pastor Jeff McCracken was dreaming of the day when mission work would become a way of life for his people. A time of serving overseas changed his life, and God was urging him to lead the Drayton church to more active mission involvement.

At the same time, without knowing his pastor's heart, Jim Johnson, a businessman in the church, sensed God moving the congregation toward orphanage ministry. He didn't know which orphanage, where, or how. He just knew that children needed help, and God was calling Drayton to take part. Next, the youth group shared with Pastor Jeff their passion for doing mission work with an orphanage in a third-world country.

The church leadership sat down with all these ideas. They decided to follow the pathway of discovery and see where He would lead them.

First, Pastor Jeff and Jim did some exploring. They met with a group in Colorado Springs to learn about training missionaries and with other organizations to learn about working with orphans. They also started praying toward the place God would lead them.

Somewhere along the way, they developed a kinship with a woman named Judy Lichter, who headed a group called Children of Promise. She recommended a few different organizations, including Go Ye Ministries. Pastor Jeff and Jim kept working to make the right missions connection. They spoke with orphanage directors in Mexico, Haiti, and Guatemala before calling me.

"This is it!" the Lord said as we finished our conversation. Jeff, Jim, and I had a real connection, and I knew the Holy Spirit was at work. When we prayed together, God added the confirmation they needed. "You understood our heartbeat to grow people," Pastor Jeff recalls. "Finding a missionary to work with was like trying to find a needle in a haystack. But when we prayed with you, it was like, 'Okay, we've got a kindred spirit.' We sensed the binding of our hearts, and when we prayed, the Holy Spirit came. That was our confirmation."

In December 2005 I went to visit the Canadian church. That

was the first of many trips to this congregation that has become my family. As Jim says, "We wanted to be part of all the highs and lows of relationship with you. We understood from the beginning that we were in it for the long haul."

I spoke in their Sunday morning service, and God came. After the service ended, people waited in line to talk and pray with me.

The church was ready to go. Even before I came to Canada, they had twenty-seven people signed up to serve in Peru. In fact, they had $25,000 raised for the trip before connecting with me. At the time, the twenty-seven people represented almost two-thirds of their congregation. Through the years, I've taken many steps of faith. But this church was taking several huge leaps at once.

Pastor Jeff put in place a solid process for church members who want to serve on mission teams. They each fill out an application and have an interview. Those who are selected go through training so that by the time they get to Peru, they're prepared for whatever God brings their way. Heather Clemmer, who has served on the team several times, says, "This is the fun and neat part – the thing that Pastor Jeff has always stressed and taught us. He doesn't want to make the trip about money but about the calling from God."

If God wants us to go, He makes sure it happens, we do what we're supposed to do.

Because of that emphasis, the team doesn't do huge fundraisers. Instead, each person sends out a letter about the trip to friends and family members. Whatever donations come in go to support the entire team. Each missionary is asked to raise at least $500, but no one misses the trip because of a lack of funds. And all the money has come in every time. "If God wants us to go, He makes sure it happens," says Heather. "We do what we're supposed to do."

When the team comes (usually once a year during February

or March), they hire women from Las Palmeras to cook and clean. That way, the missionaries are free to minister as the Lord leads. Sometimes they work with our school, going into the English classes to help teach or answering the students' questions about life in Canada. "Do you live in igloos?" someone always asks.

Because of Go Ye's strong ties to Generation of Leaders, the church has the freedom to help there in any way they can. Sometimes the teachers have the questions. And every year, after the team leaves, the teachers and students sound like our Casa kids: "When is Canada coming back?"

One of the other favorite things the Canadians do is an "Ask the Lord" or a treasure hunt. We had never heard of this before they came, but we love watching God work. An Ask the Lord is a word of knowledge where God gives insights and the team moves in response to His leading.

In an Ask the Lord, the team gathers for prayer, asking God to show them someone specific who needs ministry. Sometimes He tells them what color clothing the person they can help is wearing. Sometimes He whispers a name or a need. He always gives enough information for the team members to use in doing His work.

One day, a Canadian named Tracey felt sick, so she planned to stay back from ministry. But she joined in the Ask the Lord before the others left. God spoke to her about someone named Franco, Francisco, or Frank – she wasn't quite sure. She lay down to rest, and the team headed out without her.

First, they prayed for one woman they met and witnessed her healing. Next, they saw a couple and their son walking down the street.

"Hey, is your name Franco, or anything like that?" the team asked.

"His name is Francisco, but you can call him Frank. In Spanish, it's *Franco*."

The team couldn't believe it. This little boy had all three of the names God had shown Tracey! They were excited to pray for him and his family.

The same day, Tracey also had a vision of a woman who had lost her husband not long before. As the team moved through the community, they weren't sure where to go next. Most of the houses were empty, with parents at work and children in school. The whole team sat down to pray when a woman walked up.

"Are you census takers?" she asked.

When she found out they wanted to pray for her, tears filled her eyes. "I lost my husband a few months ago," she confessed. The team not only prayed for her but had the privilege of leading her to Christ. Every time the Canadian team comes here, we see God do amazing things. Through the years, these teams have worked to help the school, the church, and the orphanage. Before they come, I make a list of tasks that need doing. They do their best to get through my list, and the Lord provides lots of unplanned opportunities too.

On one of the final days of the church's second trip to Peru, a mother brought her children to talk about putting them in the orphanage. As one of the team members put it, she was "pretty much looking for daycare." Many of the mothers here find themselves in her situation, needing a safe place for their children to stay while they work. The mother was heartbroken at the thought of leaving her little ones.

"We're an orphanage," I explained gently. "You would have to sign off on the paperwork, and someone else could adopt your children." I have to make sure the mothers understand this before they think about leaving their children here. This time, the mother chose not to do so.

By the time we finished, the mother, the Canadian women,

and I were all crying. We all wanted to change her situation but felt helpless. We bought her some groceries and paid for a *moto* so she could take the bags of food home, but that seemed like a small gesture compared to her great need.

After the family left, I turned to the group and said, "This too is mission work. And if you don't do it, who will? I need you to come every year and bring anything you can to help these families." Few of them have missed a trip since.

The Canadians and I share a strong belief that we can bring God's light to the streets of Pacasmayo, and the relationship they have with our kids is unique. One year, they printed photos they took and helped the children make scrapbooks. These weren't just memory books, but scrapbooks of blessings. When the team presented the completed books, a different person prayed over every child, sharing words God spoke to them about that child's future. You should have seen the kids' faces. I don't think anyone who was present will ever forget that day.

Because the church and so many of its members have returned again and again, God has granted them a continuing ministry with our kids. Some of them call the Canadians *tia* or *tio* ("aunt" or "uncle"). One of our many girls from an abusive background opened right up to them, but others take longer. One teenager hardly spoke the first time they came. But by their next visit, she melted into the arms of a Canadian *tia*, Fran, telling her how scared she was, how unworthy she felt, and more.

"You're a princess," Fran reassured her. "Christ has made you worthy."

These children need someone they can trust. And the Canadians truly understand their purpose here. "Christ sends us for a reason," Fran says. "We can be that person to share the truth with them right where they need it. Then He begins the healing process. I would be down there all the time if it was what God wanted me to do!"

I need more people like Fran, and I need more churches like the one from Drayton, willing to invest in God's kingdom by helping Go Ye Ministries and our children. I will keep trusting Him to send me just the right ones.

Out of the Dust: Tony and Mary Ann Giesen's Story

Mary Ann: *The first time she came to Canada, Avis stayed in our house. My first impression of her was peace. We had the privilege of really getting to know her. I was a new Christian at the time; I came to the Lord when I was fifty-eight years old.*

Tony: *I was sixty-five before I came to know the Lord, and within a couple of months, I applied to go on a mission trip to Peru. The Lord put a verse from Jeremiah on my heart where it says to "stop murdering the innocents."*

"Lord, I haven't murdered anyone," I told Him. But the verse goes on about looking after the orphans and the widows. Now there, I could do something. He put it on my heart to build a house on the mission field so that when the workers overdo it, they could have a place to rest. And it turned out my wife had prayed for the Lord to show me something special.

We came back to Peru in March 2008 with the mission trip from our church. Again, we looked for some property. One of the pastors had built a house, and there was property available right next to him.

We started to build in January of 2009, and our house was finished in April. Ever since then, we've been coming back for five to six months a year to serve Avis and the other workers.

Mary Ann: *Avis is such an encourager. It doesn't matter who is with her, she finds good, uplifting words of encouragement.*

Kindness just flows out of her. If somebody needs money, she just opens up her heart. It's beautiful to be around her, and it just rubs off.

Tony: *She is dynamite. She completely trusts the Lord. He keeps putting her in a position that there is no money for the next month, and she has to trust in Him to make it available. For all these years she's been here, it's worked out. The Lord has come through every time.*

Sometimes that's very hard, even if you have great trust and belief and faith. If the money isn't there the day before you need it, what do you do? You keep trusting, just like the old hymn, "Trust and Obey." That's the way Avis lives. And that's the way I want to live too.

CHAPTER 20

Don't Waste Your Pain

⟨ ⟩

No part of ministry comes without a battle. I don't say that to complain, though. I know God's desires for this place and these people are great because the enemy has fought so hard against them. And the conflict began long before my work in Peru or Honduras.

For a moment, let's travel back to the garden of Eden. Do you remember the story in Genesis 3? When Eve, the woman God had created for Adam, *saw that the fruit of the tree was good for food and pleasing to the eye, and also desirable for gaining wisdom, she took some and ate it. She also gave some to her husband, who was with her, and he ate it* (Genesis 3:6).

At that point, all hell broke loose. First, the guilty pair hurried to make fig-leaf aprons. Before the fall, they were *naked, and ... felt no shame* – not ignorant, but innocent. Now, their innocence was lost. And in the loss of that innocence, they also lost the connection with God, the free communication Adam enjoyed when he walked and talked in the garden with Him (Genesis 2).

John 10:1 tells us about the one who tries to gain access to the sheep however he can. The enemy of our souls makes every attempt possible to claw his way into humanity because he has no right to our souls. But the shepherd, Scripture says, has full access to the sheep. He doesn't have to force his way into the pen. The door is open, and *the sheep listen to his voice. He calls his own sheep by name and leads them out* (John 10:3b-4). But they won't follow the stranger because they don't recognize his voice (John 10:5).

Here, Jesus shows us that the communication broken in the fall is restored when we have a relationship with Him. Satan still tries to reach us, but Christ has constant access through His Holy Spirit. I count on Him to help me through.

But I don't want to paint too rosy a picture. Go Ye Ministries has endured some difficult times. Remember the pastor who ordained me with the spirit of unity? That's the battle I've faced all the way through. I've had ministry partners hurt me in deep ways. I've experienced the pain of broken relationships and the discouragement loneliness brings.

Cancer cut short my marriage to Dean, and it's taken me a long time to feel comfortable as a single woman. I still fight feelings of being alone. For years, I prayed for a female ministry partner, but that hasn't happened. In fact, both friends I thought might serve in this way died of cancer. Although I'm close to my family, who have helped in amazing ways, they all have responsibilities back home.

Our lack of consistent covering from a church or organization has hurt us too. I sought that early on, but it never seemed to work out. So outside of our wonderful board of trustees, Go Ye Ministries has lacked partners to stand behind us and cover us spiritually, financially, and in other ways.

But every time things seem unfair, I remember Jesus. When it came to ministry, *his own did not receive him"* (John 1:11). One of His disciples betrayed Him. Another denied Him three times.

As almost any missionary will tell you, the sheer logistics of working in a foreign country can be overwhelming. Everything we try to do in Peru takes at least three times as long as it would in the United States. I go to one office, and they tell me one thing; I go to another office, and they tell me something else. A few weeks later, they send a letter telling me something completely different. And this holds true for everything from the organization that oversees the children's welfare to the local mayor's office.

From April to August of 2006, my brother Fred and his wife, Peggy, oversaw construction of our second orphanage, the set of buildings where we now house Casa de Paz (the first has become the Generation of Leaders school). We bought land from the city and thought everything was fine.

But what we didn't know was that Pacasmayo's new mayor had promised the same land to someone who helped with his campaign. Election time was near, and the man wanted to collect his debt. The whole situation almost destroyed us before we even began.

Fred, Peggy, and I were in a restaurant eating dinner when I kept hearing "Go Ye Ministries" blaring over a television hung in the corner. The mayor had brought in bulldozers to knock down a building built by people they called "invaders," those who built on land they didn't own.

But why, over the noisy background of crashing cement, did the announcer keep mentioning our ministry? It didn't take us long to put it together: Go Ye was next. In order to cover his mistake, the mayor deemed us invaders and was sending equipment to knock down the blocks we had just put in place.

It took a while to untangle the mess, but once we did, we got in touch with the San Pedro government (the equivalent of a county seat for our area) that sold us the land. In order to stop the destruction, their engineer had to approve our plans. More red tape – and more time.

Back and forth we went between the offices. In the meantime, we still had to take care of the kids, help lead the church, and keep building, building, building. It was a good thing we depended on God. Only He could give us the strength to persevere.

After a few weeks, we could move forward with the construction at last. We never did understand all the required changes, but at least our orphans would have a place to live.

Our water line at Casa de Paz has also suffered from logistical problems. We turn on our faucets and get nothing. We have a well that Emma Mier, a wonderful woman from British Columbia, paid for, but it holds salt water, so we use it only for bathing and washing clothes. Every few days, we haul drinking water from a well several miles away.

But what about city water? We used to have water from Pacasmayo, but too many people invaded the orphanage line by cutting into it to divert water to their homes. So many people eventually had free water that, although we still paid for ours, we got nothing at all.

We lived with this situation for years. We would call or go visit the local office, the city would promise us water, and nothing would happen. But the water engineer finally said if we could dig a new trench for our line, he would lay the pipe himself.

"No," my Peruvian workers said when I told them about his offer. They didn't want to cause trouble. Many of the men in the community are criminals, and our men were afraid to cross them.

But God has not given us a spirit of fear. Our kids needed water, and I was tired of waiting. "Come on, we're going to do this," I said. I got a shovel and began to dig. My friend Isabel did too.

It didn't take long before the Peruvian workers, shamefaced, joined us. The neighborhood men shouted horrible things, but we kept digging. We called the water engineer, and after he joined us, the furor died down. In only a few more weeks, we again had running water. But only a few months more, and so many people had cut into the new line that our water disappeared again. For now, we're back to hauling drinking water two or three times a week.

This may seem like a small inconvenience, but it's a costly one in terms of time, wear on our combi (the Peruvian term for a minivan), and manpower. I don't know many North Americans who would choose to bathe or wash their clothes in cold salt water, but it's our way of life. After months of watering our meager landscaping with nothing but salt water, the plants have almost all died. And we have to seal up our drinking water to keep out the dust of Las Palmeras.

Until God makes a way for fresh water to flow from our faucets again, we'll keep using other sources. I praise Him for all He gives us and for the living water He pours out in our lives.

Of course, I can't blame all our struggles on sin or Satan. Some of them come from my own mistakes or poor decisions. You may remember the story of my teaching the women of Las Palmeras to make scrubbies (nylon net scrubbers). I would pay them for their work and then take several thousand scrubbies back to the States to sell. We also made purses and learned how to crochet plastic sacks into big tote bags. Once they learn a particular craft or skill, the Las Palmeras women are very productive.

But when I travel back in the U.S., I stay busy speaking and visiting family. It was hard for me to find places to sell these crafts. My friends bought some, but the rest would end up in someone's garage. So after a while, I stopped having the women make crafts.

Later, we had a sewing opportunity. I bought $500 worth of fabric and two power machines at discount. My friend

Rachel, the woman who bought my custom bra business years ago, needed a certain kind of bra made that she couldn't find anywhere else. We tried and tried, but we couldn't get it right.

After many failed attempts, I went to see a California designer to see if he could figure it out. "This bra has all kinds of stretch," he told me. "If you buy a bolt of lace and get this pattern working, the next bolt will have just enough slack that you'll have to tweak all your patterns. I've been in the business my whole life, and I wouldn't touch this project with a ten-foot pole." He must have seen my disappointment, because he added, "But if God tells you to do it, don't listen to me."

But if God tells you to do it, don't listen to me.

I returned to Peru discouraged. We gave up on our bra-making idea, and Rachel found someone else. So we had three fancy sewing machines, a bolt of material, and nothing to show for it (or sew with it). It seemed my ideas for empowering the women all ended in disappointment.

What does God say about situations like this? He tells me not to worry about anything, but to pray about everything (Philippians 4:6). I've made more mistakes than I realize, but every once in a while, I do something right. He uses our mistakes, especially when they happen out of ignorance. And most of the time, I'm as ignorant as they come.

God is making something beautiful out of our sewing machine story even now. Our friend Isabel learned to sew on a treadle machine and has now mastered our electric models. She spends some of her time each week teaching our older girls to use the machine and embroider. We hope to offer the items online, which should help solve some of our sales problems. Most of all, we'll keep trusting God to use everything – even our mistakes – to bring Him glory.

My life has never looked like a fairy tale. But I've seen how God uses every bit of it, even the pain and the problems. Every experience I've had, good or bad, is an offering. And God will take everything you've experienced and use it in His plan for you too. He will never waste your pain.

Out of the Dust: Pete Lupton's Story

I don't remember the first time I met Avis. But one thing I do know is that I was supposed to go to Peru since forever.

I knew Avis had an orphanage. And when she came to our church (in Drayton, Canada) and Pastor Jeff set up that first mission trip, I said, "I'm going to try to go."

Lots of people wanted to go, but the church could only take so many. I was a new member and didn't even know the real reason I wanted to go so much. But when I walked in the door for the interview with the missions committee, God spoke to my heart: "You dummy, you're an orphan. You know first-hand what it's like to be in an orphanage."

Now, I don't have many memories of those days [in the orphanage], *and my adoptive parents are fantastic. But I told the committee what God had laid on my heart: I wanted to go and give back.*

There in Pacasmayo, I felt completely at ease. I've been there three times now. My wife has served there, and our oldest daughter has been there five times. We feel like it's a second home.

It's amazing the way you go there with preconceived ideas about what's going to happen. Some things do happen, but more often than not, they don't.

When we go to Peru, we do whatever Avis needs. She's like a mother figure. And if I ever try to praise or thank her for the amazing things she's done, she'll say, "It's not me, it's God." I try to tell her that without feet on the ground, God can't accomplish

His work. But every time, she reminds me, "Remember, it's not me, it's God."

I could go on for hours about how going on these mission trips has changed me, my daughters, my wife, and our relationship. Having known Avis and seen the work there, we've all come to realize there's more to life than punching a clock or working and having a structured life.

Whether in Canada or on the field in Peru, Avis never pressures anyone. She doesn't dictate or give orders. She just puts the need out there and asks if she can count on our support. "If you can give, that would be awesome," she says. And if you can't give, she loves you anyway.

I'm a police officer, so I've seen lots of things. Ten years ago, I never would have prayed for anyone who slighted me. Now, not only do I do that, but I've passed on the practice to my girls. I think they're both better for knowing Avis and her amazing relationship with God.

After everything God's done for me, giving back seems like the least I can do.

CHAPTER 21

From Four to Nine

⟨decorative flourish⟩

Ask any good mother which is her favorite child, and she'll tell you, "All of them."

At Casa de Paz, all our children are our favorites too. They all have qualities that make them precious. But the longer they stay with us, the more we love them, and the more we miss them when they're gone.

For our staff, the adoption of a child or sibling group is both happy and sad. We're always happy for the children being adopted. And we're always a little sad for ourselves, because adoption usually means we lose contact with children who have become such a part of our lives.

Not long ago, the atmosphere at Casa de Paz swirled with rumors and excitement. For almost two years, a family from Blue Springs, Missouri, had been trying to adopt a sibling group of five. And for almost two years, we'd seen the likelihood of the adoption shift back and forth. The judge had approved it. No, he hadn't. There was a major holdup. No, there wasn't.

Throughout the time, we kept praying for the family and for the children: Yhonson, Gerson, Betsi, Joel, and Sibila. People in the United States were praying too. And now, it looked as though God was finally saying yes.

We couldn't help but think back to the time nearly seven years earlier when this little family arrived after their court-ordered placement. The youngest, Sibila, was not even two years old, and the oldest, Yhonson, was ten. They came from a small village high in the mountains. Relatives tried to avoid sending them away, but no one had time or money to take care of all five. So our Casa de Paz family received them with joy.

And now, it looked as though God was finally saying yes.

About ten months after the siblings' arrival, the orphanage had an outbreak of tuberculosis. The intake doctors had told us this little family was clear of the disease, but they were wrong. After the diagnosis, Gerson, then seven years old, spent two weeks in the hospital for treatment, and all his siblings also tested positive for TB. To fulfill Peruvian law, we had to take them downtown every day to swallow their medicine under a doctor's watchful eye. And we often had to make the two-hour trip to Trujillo to have them checked at a clinic there. But with God's help; good medicine; and lots of tender, loving care, we all survived.

As months and then years passed, more and more people grew to love these kids. Yhonson stood out at school in almost every way. He excelled in both athletics and academics. Accustomed to watching out for his younger siblings, he served as a role model at school and at the orphanage. Everyone loved him, and he relished rather than resented his leadership role.

Gerson, the second boy, had an equally sweet personality. We were concerned about him, though, because he had trouble walking. His calf muscles seemed to tighten up with exertion and cause great pain. We took him to doctor after doctor who ran test after test. Their conclusion? *"Psychologica"* (psychological).

According to the Peruvian medical experts, the trouble was all in his head.

I knew Gerson too well to believe this was true. I watched him struggle to play soccer and run with the other kids. He never gave up or admitted anything was wrong. I watched him fight back the tears when his legs wouldn't do what he wanted. *All in his head*? I didn't think so. But this gave us another reason to pray for the adoption to go through. Maybe the doctors in the United States could find the right answer.

Betsi, Joel, and little Sibila could also benefit from America's many advantages. We would have loved to keep them in Peru, but we couldn't change our desires or prayers for these children. What would God do?

In the spring of 2012, when it looked as though the adoption was progressing well, the court told us we still needed birth certificates for a couple of the kids. In order to get them, we had to travel to the little mountain village where they were born. After one false start, Gina (the orphanage director) and I set off on a true adventure.

First, we took the bus to Trujillo, two hours away. From there, we took another bus that traveled through the night. For the first four hours, it rumbled along on pavement, but for the next four, the driver navigated a winding dirt road high in the mountains.

When the bus dropped us off in a small mountain town just before sunrise, we knew what we had to do. Those who had made this trip before told us we could rent a private car to take us four more hours to a place where we could rent mules for the final four-hour leg of our journey. We were exhausted, but we hadn't come this far to leave without the documents we needed.

But first, we smelled coffee. We traced it to a small wooden building where an old lady offered home-baked bread. She could scramble an egg for us too. So there we sat, trying to get our bearings and figure out the next step.

We walked through the streets a short time later, looking for someone to help. Gina kept asking people how we could rent a car, and everyone told us to hitch a ride with one of the mine workers. Of course, *hitching* meant "pay them money so they'll take you."

It didn't take too long to find someone who would set up a ride, but the departure time was 2:00 a.m. We found a small hotel where, exhausted, we lay down with our clothes on. We got up in the middle of the night and crossed the little square to wait for the truck that would be our taxi.

While we waited, the woman who arranged our ride heard us talking. When she found out why we needed the birth certificates, she said, "I have friends who are teachers up there. They come out once a month, and they're due in three days." She paused a moment. "I could get a message to them to bring out the birth certificates. Why don't you save yourselves a trip?"

It sounded crazy. We already had the ride set up, and even if she could arrange to get the certificates, we'd have to wait for them. But just as our ride pulled up to the square, God spoke into my spirit: *Don't get in the truck.*

So we didn't. After we told the driver our plans had changed, he slammed the door in our faces and pulled back onto the road. We trudged back across the square and went straight back to our motel bed.

Did we do the right thing? we wondered in the morning. But two days later, when the teachers came out with the kids' birth certificates, we were overjoyed. The money we paid for their delivery service was less than what we'd have spent to go the rest of the way ourselves. And now we only had two more bus rides to get back to the orphanage.

I've had so many times like this in the years I've been in Peru, times where I didn't know where to go or what to do and God put exactly the right person in front of me at exactly the right time. Times where I made a decision that seemed to make no sense just because God told me to do it. Times where something looked impossible, but God made it happen.

The next impossible task was finalizing the kids' adoption. At the time, Kevin Guier, a long-term volunteer, was working here. Like the Sterlings, his family lived in Blue Springs, Missouri. In fact, his parents had adopted two girls from our orphanage the year before. Kevin now took on the job of running interference for this new adoption. Various authorities within the Peruvian government told him it couldn't go through at least a dozen times.

Besides the normal obstacles, Scott and Lauren Sterling had a special problem: Lauren's age. Peruvian law requires the adoptive mother to be at least eighteen years older than the children she adopts. Although Lauren was both stepmom to Scott's teenage daughter, Logan, and mom to their biological daughter, Laney, she didn't meet that requirement. More than once, the officials told the Sterlings they would make an exception. And more than once, the officials changed their minds.

The months went by. The Sterlings pressed forward through every setback. They were now Skyping with "their" kids, who already called them Mom and Dad, once a week or more. And they also had two attorneys in Lima working on their behalf. Every time the government ruled against the adoption, the lawyers went right back in and filed paperwork to reverse the decision. They were willing to fight on their clients' behalf and for the kids' right to have the life and family they needed.

By Thanksgiving 2012, after nearly two years of emotion-racked waiting, the Sterlings received the call. They could travel to Peru and finalize the adoption. "You're good to go," the coordinator said. "You can come now if you want, or you can wait until after the first of the year. Let us know when you buy your plane tickets."

Weary of all the waiting, they chose to complete their family right away. Scott, Lauren, and little Laney (Logan couldn't leave her college classes) left the United States on November 25, knowing the process could still take a while. They landed in Lima after midnight and squeezed in only four hours of sleep before an early-morning meeting with their attorneys. The family flew to Trujillo later that same day, then took two different vans to reach Casa de Paz and their long-awaited children.

I left for the United States and some needed medical treatment earlier that month, so I missed this final step of the adoption. But once I returned, the staff gave me the full report. They said the mama was so young and the papa so handsome. The Peruvian kids all fell in love with their new family. They spent time playing together, showing off their school and their activities, and buying brand-new clothes (a rarity in our hand-me-down world) for the entire family.

Just a few days after Scott, Lauren, and Laney arrived, Casa de Paz gave the five children a huge send-off party. Amid the tears, prayers, and well-wishes, the brand-new Sterlings said good-bye to the people and place that had housed them for seven years and hello at last to life with a forever-family.

Out of the Dust: Lauren Sterling's Story

We couldn't believe we had the opportunity to appear on the popular television show The View in February 2013. But there's more to our adoption story than we could tell there.

It all began through our church, Gateway, which has a strong emphasis on adoption and foster care. Lots of families have adopted, including Kelly and Lisa Guier, who brought home two sisters from Casa de Paz about a year before we got our kids.

In January 2010, the Guiers' grown son, Kevin, who was serving at Casa de Paz as a volunteer, sent out an email to a handful of couples in our church. "We need a Mommy and Daddy," it began, followed by a brief explanation and photo of each child.

My husband, Scott, and I looked at the letter and thought, "Wow! These kids are beautiful. Someone should adopt them!" At the time, we had a one-year-old, Laney, and a sixteen-year-old, Logan, Scott's daughter from a previous marriage. We didn't give the email a second thought.

But by March, I felt restless, wanting my faith to grow. Longing to be a part of something bigger than myself, I tagged along with some friends on a mission trip to an orphanage in Guatemala. I'd closed my heart to adoption, but after spending a week with a hundred twenty or so kids, something changed.

This wasn't a mission trip where I got rejuvenated. Instead, I got wrecked.

I kept thinking, "My kid's at home with a million people who want to watch her while I'm gone, and some of these kids may never get families." I couldn't figure out what to do with what I saw.

Next, I went on vacation with my parents and read a book called Reckless Faith. The author talks about trusting that God sometimes asks us to do things that don't make any sense. Someone brought up the email about the five kids, and before I knew it, my friends and I were discussing how some of us could take the boys and some the girls.

Scott laughed, but he didn't act like I was crazy – not all the way, anyway. I didn't know how it could work, but these kids stayed in my mind and on my heart.

We happened to be making the big decision right then about whether or not to get a mini-van, which we'd never owned before.

I didn't want to limit our family size by the size of our vehicles. And I also didn't want to split those five kids.

They need a family, I thought. I gotta figure out if that's us.

When Logan, our teenager, first heard us mention the possibility of adoption, her first words were, "Are you serious?" But in the middle of worship one day, she came up to me, so passionate. "Lauren," she said. "I think we're supposed to do this."

Of course that made me cry. I had messaged Kevin's mom, Lisa, on Facebook earlier that day and said, "This is crazy, but would you be willing to meet with me before church sometime? I want to talk through some things with you."

We ended up meeting that same day. And I had some questions. Sure, Kevin was in love with the kids, but why America? Is America the answer, or do they just need financial support? Is taking them out of Peru even the answer? I knew Lisa would tell me straight up.

But first, she cried too. She loved those kids as much as Kevin did. Her take on the situation was that the opportunities were limited. No, America isn't the answer for everybody, and people can and do have great lives elsewhere. But the opportunities for these kids to become what they wanted just didn't exist in Peru. The older ones would be college-age soon, but could they go? And one of the boys needed medical attention. The orphanage staff had done as much as they could to help him, but he needed more.

Easter Sunday we went to church, and as usual, I couldn't stop thinking about the kids. "Resurrection is all about new life," I told Scott, reminding him of his promise to pray about adoption.

I wanted an immediate answer like, "Yes, let's do it!" What he gave me was much more typical: silence. But later that day, while we were at his parents' for Easter brunch, he turned to me and said, "Okay, I'm willing."

That answer came because he had wrestled with God during the service. "I kept asking, 'What about the money?' and 'What about the house? What if these kids don't even want us to adopt them?"' Scott told me later. "It was as though God turned on the intercom and said, 'I didn't ask about the money, the house, or the kids and their response. I asked if you were willing.'"

Scott was. And so was I.

Later that week, we asked Kevin to reach out to Yhonson and see what he thought about our idea. Before Kevin could get the words out, Yhonson said, "Yes, I want a family."

One by one, as Yhonson told his brothers and sisters, they all agreed. Kevin sent an email to let us know, "Yes, they want you." We went out to breakfast that day and just sat there crying.

They chose us too. That's a really big deal.

Prepublication Updates

During the Sterlings' appearance on *The View* (February 6, 2013), the president of Avila University in Kansas City, Missouri, surprised them with $500,000 in scholarships for all seven of their children. They also received a new washer and dryer and some other gifts to help make their transition from a family of four to one of nine easier. The Sterlings and their adoption journey were also featured in a documentary on national Peruvian television.

The Sterling family has now transitioned from nine to ten with the birth of a healthy Cruz Daniel Sterling on May 28, 2014. Congratulations!

The Sterling family shares their adoption story on ABC's *The View*: http://youtu.be/9BruFzYozKs

CHAPTER 22

Poder de Mujeres

⟨⟩─────────⟨⟩

Ever since God led us to plant our ministry in Pacasmayo, He has led me to spend most of my time here in Peru. I've been so busy with the church, school, and orphanage that I haven't done much ministry elsewhere. I will transition to doing more traveling and speaking again, often in the United States.

When I'm in Peru, though, I plan to spend more and more time expanding my ministry to the women of this country. Someone has to be a voice to reach them.

Some of these women live in huts along the Amazon. Others live in tiny villages so high up in the mountains that no one knows they're there. And of course, still others make their homes of cardboard and crumbling block here in Las Palmeras, the community built on the dump.

Someone has to link back to these women to let them know Jesus loves them and they matter to Him. And that's what I try to do with the weekly Bible study I hold when I'm in Peru. In fact, Las Palmeras is the home of one of my most treasured places of ministry.

When I first started my work here, I didn't know the language at all. To this day, because of my dyslexia, I don't speak or understand it well. I get by on a mixture of prayer, sign language, fractured Spanish, and help from others who know a few words of English. But I believe we who have so much from God have a responsibility to share with these women who have so little. And in turn, they share with us. But He is the only true giver.

He used my growing-up years to teach me many important lessons, and one of those was that money doesn't define who you are. Understanding this helped move me from feeling insignificant to knowing my true value. God, not man, is my provider. That's what I want these women to know. I tell them, "Just because you don't have money doesn't mean you're broke. You can hope, dream, think, and feel. You have possibilities. And in the Lord, you always have hope."

Hope is what we bring with us every week when we go out from Casa de Paz to lead a women's Bible study a mile or two away at the far end of Las Palmeras. While we meet in a home, a volunteer and one or two of the older girls from the orphanage hold Kids' Club outside.

Our Kids' Club consists of a simple Bible program with a story, a craft, and a much-anticipated snack. As soon as our combi pulls up, children stream from all over the neighborhood to join us. Sometimes we've had as many as sixty or more attend.

A smaller group of women (eight to twelve) meets in Flor's home for the Bible study. Her house looks like most of the others in Las Palmeras, with its packed dirt floor, walls of cardboard lined with woven bamboo mats, and single light bulb hanging overhead. Plastic tacked to the ceiling adds a thin layer of protection, and hanging plastic and mats separate the house into makeshift rooms. But to me, it's the home of my dear friend.

We cram plastic stools into her small front room and study a Christian book together. Flor reads the chapter aloud in Spanish. After every few paragraphs, we stop to discuss what we've read. I'm the Bible study leader, but Flor often leads when I can't attend. Our time together is simple but special. Since this group began meeting, I've really seen a change in the women. They're stronger. They walk straighter and seem to think more of themselves. They're kinder to each other and to their husbands. Some have taken big steps like baptism. But almost all keep coming to our study. I tell them "Poder de Mujeres!" or "Women Power!" They know I mean the power we find in Christ. His grace is all-sufficient, and He gives us the power to follow even when times are tough.

The women of Las Palmeras are a special part of my life. In my years in Peru, I've had the privilege of ministering to more than one group of women here and seen them grow in the Lord. The current Bible students represent a new generation who moved in only a couple of years ago, although I've known Flor longer than the rest.

When I can, I like to have these Bible study friends join me in other activities outside of our study time. I decided to take as many of them as I could to a small shopping mall in Trujillo not long ago. Most of the women had never been to a place like this before, and they were so excited they talked about it for weeks ahead of time. By car or bus, the mall is about two hours away. But by experience, the distance is much greater.

Riding on an escalator was one of the first new experiences of our trip. To reach the housewares section in one store, my sisters in Christ climbed onto the moving steps with some fear. "Look at those pots and pans!" they exclaimed, fingering the shiny metal. They loved everything about our trip, and I loved seeing a familiar place with their fresh eyes.

We later ate lunch in the food court, another new adventure. The women tucked the paper coffee cups into their purses so they could use them again. I hadn't thought to explain that most people just throw them away. And we all enjoyed the large plates of chicken and *papas fritas* (fried potatoes), a common restaurant treat.

Because of some generous donations, I had enough to give each of my friends one hundred soles (about forty dollars) for shopping. Although they enjoyed looking at and exclaiming over the items in the stores, all anyone bought in the end was groceries. These wise stewards took the food back home to their families and saved the rest of their money.

But tight budgets didn't keep these women from having fun. While we ate lunch, we talked, laughed, and sang together. I guess you could say we laughed our way all through the mall. On our way back to Pacasmayo that afternoon, I thanked God for the sweet day He had given us and for reminding me to see the joy in the little things.

Tight budgets didn't keep these women from having fun.

I would love to offer more opportunities for the women of this community. We have an experiment in place at Flor's house, in fact. A couple of years ago, Go Ye Ministries invested some of our money and helped her set up a little *bodega* (store) in her home. We explained about profit and loss and how at first she would need to reinvest most of her profit to build up the stock of supplies. Now, her store has grown, and although it's still in her home, she offers many more items for sale. Her husband also takes some of the things she makes and sells them in downtown Pacasmayo.

I love seeing Flor and the others mature from week to week and month to month as God works in their lives. You see, these women are not much different from you and me. They love the Lord, they love their families, and they like to have fun together. Each one has changed because of Jesus. They may live amid blowing dust on the top of a landfill, but as they come to know Him more, He is bringing them into His good plans for their lives.

Isabel's Story

I have learned much, so I give much. But Sister Avis is more than a good teacher. She's a great example too. She preached the truth about Jesus to me, and now I preach to some of my friends who aren't Christians. I tell them how big God is. They remember me back before I was a Christian, when I used bad language and was always scared. But now, I am smiling, happy, and I have peace from God. I'm able to live my life "One Day at a Time," like the song we sing when we meet together.

My close friends who come to the Bible study and I, we all have different problems. But we laugh and smile, and we just deal with today, no more. We don't think about the past or worry about the future.

I like to minister in the women's prison in Trujillo. The women there tell me, "Isabel, please visit us!" So I go and preach to them whenever I can. One of the women I led to Christ asked me to pray for her when she was going in front of the judge [for a parole hearing]. She had been sentenced to twenty years. So I prayed for her, and she said, "The bars, they don't imprison me. I am really free. So it doesn't matter what the judge decides." When she had her hearing, the judge released her after she had served only six years.

"What are you going to do when you get out?" I asked.

"I'm going to look for a church for my children and me." It meant a lot to me that God used me to make a difference in this woman's life.

I am no longer garbage. I am new. I am a strong woman. I am not scared. I can work, I can do it. Whatever the situation, I can handle it because I know God is my strength.

CHAPTER 23

Partners in Ministry

❦

For the last few years, I've felt like my life is changing again. It's time for a shift. First of all, God has brought me some wonderful new partners in ministry, Jake and Maggie Hiebert. This wonderful young couple and their children, Karlita and Mateo, came to us from a small church in Drayton, Ontario. Jake first came to Casa de Paz on one of the church's mission trips in the spring of 2011. The next year, Maggie came along too. They both grew up in Mexico and sensed God might be calling them to serve here.

Jake had a good job back in Ontario, where he planned to build a bigger, nicer home for their family. But obeying God was more important to the Hieberts than a beautiful home. Once they confirmed their calling, things moved fast – or as fast as they can when government red tape is involved. Jake quit his job, they sold their house, and by the fall of 2012, they landed in Peru. When they arrived, Maggie was pregnant with their third child, and she had already decided to stay in her new country for the delivery.

That she would choose to have her baby in Peru meant so much to the women here. And that's just the way this family has fit in. Jake is such a great example for the boys, always fixing something and jumping in wherever we need help. And everyone loves Maggie and the children (including baby Tahlia) too. They've fit in better than I thought possible, and they love the people here the same way I do. I feel more confident going back to the U.S. now, knowing they care so much and are always trying to help.

Although I'm still on the board, I've stepped down as the head of Go Ye Ministries to let Jake take charge. That way, when I'm back in the United States speaking and sharing about our ministry, he'll have the freedom to make decisions to keep things moving forward.

We couldn't survive at Go Ye without our volunteers, some short-term and some long-term. You've read some of their stories, and I want to tell about a few who have served here in the recent past.

Bruce Goulding, a Canadian, came to us in a truly amazing way. For many years, he had the idea that he would one day serve children overseas. "When I went to bed at night, I would always think of those children on the streets," he said. "One of the best gifts you can give kids is security."

For many years, Bruce was busy just making a living. An industrial plumber, he kept the dream in his heart that one day he would fulfill some kind of mission. But just when or where, he didn't know.

The answer came to him one day when he was watching the popular Ontario-based television show *100 Huntley Street*. By this time, Bruce had retired from his job and was ready to go wherever God led. "I knew I was going in the summer, but not when, where, or how. I was watching for a jump-off point to figure out how it was all going to work out," he explained. "One day, I saw you on the program talking about the orphanage you had in Peru. I sent you an email, and we started communicating."

Soon, Bruce was on the field at Casa de Paz. He watched me on the program in May 2010, and joined us at Casa de Paz that July. "The Spirit was so strong once I got to Peru," he said. "Until I got to Pacasmayo, I had tears running down my face. There was no doubt in my mind that what I was doing was right."

Bruce stayed in one of the volunteer apartments at Casa de Paz until late October, long enough for the children to capture his heart. He went home to Saskatchewan for only three weeks, then returned to Peru for four months. After that, he went back to Canada and sold many of his possessions so he could be here long-term. Today, he serves in nearby Trujillo, but he stayed with us on and off for almost three years.

During his time at Go Ye Ministries, Bruce did all kinds of things. He provided security, watching to make sure our kids were safe and checking out any problems or potential intruders. He could (and did) fix almost anything, from helping put new doors on our cottages to hauling water for us and more. For a while, he even taught English at our Generation of Leaders school.

But for Bruce, the most important aspect of his work here was his ministry to our children. "Whatever happens to these kids happens to me too," he would say. He loved seeing them smile and was fiercely protective of each one. "Kids can go either way," he said. "If we can encourage them that they can make up their own mind, and make sure they realize they really are just as valuable as any other human being, they'll start to think that way."

But the best part about having Bruce here was that he loved the kids as much as I do. "If there was ever a threat in the Bible," he said, "it's a threat about offending one of the children – the least of these. They are jewels in the Savior's crown." He still comes back to visit often.

Mandy Kauer of Wisconsin was another long-term volunteer

who blessed us for almost two years with her smile, hard work, and love for the children. She is a special education teacher who first served at Casa de Paz as part of an internship for her degree at Moody Bible Institute. After she graduated, I emailed her about the possibility of coming back to teach English.

"A couple years before, I almost quit school to serve there," Mandy said. "So now that I was finished, I told God, 'Here's my degree, here's my time' – I just dedicated it to Him. And He flung the doors to return wide open."

While she was here, Mandy showed her dedication to both God and our kids. No matter what we threw at her, she accepted the challenge. For a while, she was teaching school during the day and serving as housemother at night. Several Peruvian moms work as housemothers for our children, but they need nighttime relief. So volunteers like Mandy come in, cook dinner, help with homework, supervise showers, and get the kids to bed on time.

Mandy would also get the children up and ready for school in the morning before returning to her volunteer apartment for a few hours' sleep. Then she would walk over to teach English at our school. It was a crazy schedule, especially when the judge sent us a baby boy with brain damage who ended up in Mandy's house. She was the housemother for twelve to fourteen boys most of the time she was here.

Mandy also helped start the Kids' Club we run alongside the women's Bible study in Las Palmeras. "It's all the Lord," she said. "We did a Christmas party out there a couple of years ago where we gave out presents. After that, in January or February, we decided to try doing the Kids' Club. We got all excited about the possibilities and spent lots of time praying and preparing.

"The first time we held it, two kids showed up. We couldn't believe it: all that work and two kids! But the next week, a few more came. And before long, kids were coming from everywhere.

It's a transient neighborhood, but when some families moved away, we would have new kids coming in to take their places."

The first or second week after they began, Mandy planned to share the gospel with the children at Kids' Club. But then God convicted her: *Have you made sure everyone in your house knows the gospel?*

That night, she gathered the boys and took them through a small tract. One, who struggled with anger, said, "No, no. I'm not a Christian" and prayed to receive Christ. "I almost couldn't believe it," said Mandy.

Today, Mandy is back in Wisconsin working as a special education teacher and preparing for her upcoming marriage. But she still has a heart for missions and for the children of Casa de Paz. Before she left, she told me, "[Volunteering there was] lonely at times and lots of hard work, but I love these kids. I just feel like the Lord does extra-special things for them."

Would the Lord want you to come help us at Go Ye Ministries as either a short- or long-term volunteer? I don't know. But since the beginning of my time here, I've seen our ministry as a foundation for other people to grow in their lives and form ministries of their own. So I don't mind when people serve for a while and then move on. In fact, I expect it. God told me long ago that we would be a platform from which other people could launch.

As you read this, if you sense the Lord moving, I invite you to come down here and get your feet wet. God will work on you as you serve the people. He'll show you what's next.

And don't be afraid to come. Remember, I had every reason you can think of to stay home. Some of my disabilities kept me from working in the United States, but they also freed me to serve here. Like you, I've been through hard times and tough experiences. I've made decisions I regret and some I don't regret at all.

I have learned that every experience – the good ones and the bad ones – is a jewel I can offer to the Lord. And God will take the jewels in your life and use them in His plan for you. As I wrote earlier, don't waste your pain – but don't stay locked up in it either.

That little girl of long ago who moved from place to place, who suffered the unspeakable but loved her family no matter what, still lives inside of me. And so does the strong Jesus who enables me to do all things.

But I'm not the only one. I'm not the only wounded warrior fighting kingdom battles. And I'm not the only one God has called or commissioned.

If He's not calling you to Peru or to partner with Go Ye Ministries, I understand. No one can walk out your calling but you. Just make sure to remain connected with Him. That way, no matter where or how He uses you, you will help bring others out of the dust – and into a whole new life.

Out of the Dust: Kevin Guier's Story

I first met Avis during winter break of my junior year in college, when I sat next to her on an airplane. I had already gone to Peru twice with my church in Blue Springs, Missouri. This time I was going back with a friend on Christmas break. Avis was very talkative and funny. She looked at me and said, "Are you a missionary?"

"I don't know if I'd call myself that, but I'm in Peru to do mission work," I said.

"I knew it! You look like a missionary!"

Avis then began to tell me all about her orphanage in Pacasmayo, leaving me with the thought that I should come the next summer and teach English at her school. Over the next few months, I prayed about it a lot. That summer, I went, and one of my best friends came with me. We worked and taught English for two and a half months.

For the first couple of weeks, as planned, we helped out the English teacher already in place. But she had to leave the country suddenly due to a family illness. Just like that, we were in charge of the English classes. Teaching is not my forte, but it worked out really well. It was an awesome experience.

No one can walk out your calling but you.

While we were there, I pretty much fell in love with the city and the Casa kids. Almost every night, we would go over to the kids' houses and hang out, eat dinner, help with homework, and play games until they had to go to bed. We also took the kids out to the beach or to different fast-food restaurants. We liked to do fun stuff with them whenever we got the chance.

When I came back again, it was over Christmas break of my senior year. I brought my parents, and they met the two girls they ended up adopting. During that time, I talked with Avis, telling her I wanted to come back and help with the business part of things.

I came down the week after I graduated and stayed for about three years. During that time, my role was constantly changing as I adjusted to what most needed to be done.

The most memorable thing about my time there was the relationship I built with all the kids. I actually became like a father figure to most of them. That made it harder to come back to the United States because I felt like I lost twenty-five kids.

Overall, I felt like I grew as a person while at Casa de Paz. Even if you come only for a few months, I can't recommend the volunteer experience enough. I felt like it changed me as a person in all facets of my life.

Epilogue: Go Ye

⟨ ～～～ ⟩

It has been almost two years since Marti came to Peru for the first time to begin work on our book, and much has happened since that time.

If you're reading this, that means we finished. And if that's true, I'll spend more time in North America telling what Jesus can do through a willing heart. Through sales of *Out of the Dust,* I hope to earn much-needed funds for Go Ye Ministries and Casa de Paz.

As you read in the book, I've searched for years for the right ministry partners to continue what God used me to begin here in Peru. Praise the Lord, He sent me the perfect couple in Jake and Maggie Hiebert, whose story we shared in Chapter 23.

Not long ago, God also sent us Tammy Dicken from Tennessee. Giving up her job as a research nurse, she moved to Pacasmayo as a full-time volunteer and teaches English in our Generation of Leaders school. She is also helping some of the local women fulfill our long-held dream of a sewing business, Creating Hope. The business will teach skills and provide a better way of life along with raising money for Go Ye. You can purchase handmade dresses, purses, and slippers through our online store (see address at the end of this section).

God continued to bless us when He sent Jana and Wayne Salley, also from Tennessee, to help set up speaking engagements and promote our book. It is a blessing to work with people who love Jesus.

As we shared throughout the book, we'd love to have your help in whatever way God directs. If you feel led to pray, give, or come serve alongside us, please check out the contact and other information at the end of this section.

An update on our Casa kids: two of our young ladies are attending college, and several will turn eighteen in a year or so, with bright futures stretching before them. Praise God! What a blessing to see them grow up and continue serving Him.

We hope to make *Out of the Dust* available in Spanish as well as in English in both print and e-book formats. My desire is to share Jesus in North and South America and wherever He leads. I hope we'll meet somewhere along the way. And even if we don't, I'll see you in heaven!

Blessings,
Avis Goodhart
Pacasmayo, Peru

Contact Information

Go Ye Ministries
P.O. Box 1034
Prairie Grove, AR 72753

Website: goye-ministries.com:

Avis: avisgoodhart@gmail.com
Jake: hiebert83@gmail.com

Social Media Related to Go Ye Ministries

Creating Hope Web Store:
http://www.goyeministriescreatinghope.com/

Heart of an Orphan Blog:
www.hiebert5inperu.blogspot.com

Steps on the Journey Blog:
www.tdheartnurse.com

Facebook, In Jesus' Name Amen:
https://www.facebook.com/casadepazperu

Facebook, Out of the Dust:
www.facebook.com/outofthedustbook

Faithful Fifty

Just as stones are needed to build a strong foundation, Go Ye Ministries is looking for faithful people to donate a monthly gift of $50, $100, or $150. Each $50 represents a stone to build our firm foundation. How many stones would God have you commit to give? For more information, check out the Faithful Fifty link on our website (http://goye-ministries.com/how-to-help/faith-fifty/).

ABOVE: Day in the park, December, 1954, Miller family: Times are good; we have a nice house for the moment. Bottom (L to R) Carol, George, Fred. Top (L to R) Avis, Art, Dad (Bob), Elsie (Mom), Rada, Bobby. Avis had third-degree burns on her legs.

BELOW: Team with shoeboxes and medical supplies, airport, early 2001: Before 9/11, each team member took two large bins of shoeboxes, medicine, Bibles, and other supplies on all of our mission trips.

ABOVE: Children waiting for medicine: Children from a local kindergarten class in Pacasmayo came with their teacher to get vitamins and medicine for worms on one of the trips we made to Pacasmayo before we started building.

BELOW: Medical Team on Amazon with drum: Going from Iquitos to San Juan on the Amazon to do a medical clinic and share the good news. The man (center) will beat the drum as we go to let the villagers know we are arriving.

ABOVE: Dr. Kim on the Amazon: Dr. Kim treating the people of San Juan, downriver from Iquitos, Peru. All the houses were built on stilts in the water and reached by canoe. Many people here asked Jesus into their hearts.

ABOVE: Floating house on Amazon: Some houses are built on large logs joined together like a raft. They bob up and down with the waves of the river.

ABOVE: Hammocks hanging on the open deck of a *lancha* (boat with a paddle wheel): On this trip, we traveled three days downriver from Iquitos, Peru to Leticia, Colombia. Fred showed the JESUS Film on the lancha.

BELOW: Lancha we took downriver: There are little banana trees on the roof being taken to a plantation; several bulls in an open pen on the lower deck; and two hundred people in the open-air middle deck which was our home for three days. One of our team members is standing in the front watching all the action.

ABOVE: Amazon village: Fred and men digging a well. It is the dry season, so you can see the stilts on which the houses are built. During the rainy season the houses stand in water and the people get from house to house by canoe.

RIGHT: Fred and men digging well in Amazon: Fred dug five different wells along the Amazon. You might not think wells would be needed here, but there is no clean drinking water.

LEFT: Avis preaching in Manaus, Brazil; August 2001: Here, I spoke in the same clothes I wore for four days because I did not have a Brazilian visa and was stopped when boarding my flight in Miami. I had to wait to enter the country and arrived just in time to speak.

BELOW: Lorene and Fred loading shoeboxes: Lorene assembled thousands of shoeboxes. Each contained an outfit, new underwear, hygiene supplies, toys, candy, a Jesus coloring book, and school supplies. She could fit more into one box than you would believe possible, all of it good, clean, and packed with love. As she filled each box, Lorene prayed for the child who would receive it.

ABOVE: Children with shoeboxes: These children in the mountains of Peru are walking home with their shoebox gifts.

BELOW: Our church, Marcos 16:15: The church was the first building we built in Peru (2003). I was the pastor for the first three years because no one else was available. The church began with the thirty people who got saved at the church groundbreaking ceremony.

ABOVE: Casa de Paz, exterior view: Casa de Paz is as big as one city block, so it is hard to get a picture. We cleared off a place in the dump to build.

BELOW: Casa de Paz, aerial view: Casa de Paz taken from the top of our school building. Our landscaping is the only green in all of Las Palmeras.

ABOVE: Casa de Paz, kids playing in front of house: Kids learn quickly that they are safe here.

BELOW: Casa de Paz, kids on bikes: We only had five bikes for forty kids, but they had a great time.

ABOVE: Generation of Leaders school: We built the school to meet the educational needs of our kids. They learn English and computer skills in addition to other school subjects. Our motto is "Learning for World Changers."

BELOW: Ron Mainse, Avis Goodhart, and Moira Brown on the set of *100 Huntley Street*, May 3, 2010.

ABOVE: Girl Time, Avis and Casa girls: The older girls and I had a tea party in my small (fifteen- by sixteen-foot) apartment and enjoyed spending time together.

RIGHT: Avis and Milagros: Milagros is our oldest Casa kid. She came to us very broken with her four-day-old son. She is an amazing young woman who, through Jesus, has taken every small opportunity and built on it. Milagros speaks fluent English and is in her fourth semester at the university with the goal of becoming a psychologist.

ABOVE: Store we started in Flor's house: We invested in the startup stock for the store, and now it has grown. We also invested in a store for Yolanda, and it, too, is doing well.

BELOW: Women's Bible study at Flor's house: We meet every Saturday for Bible study and fellowship. These women live in homes made of bamboo, cardboard, and plastic with dirt floors and no running water, but they are rich in Jesus.

ABOVE: Mandy giving out drinks and cookies in Kids' Club: One of three groups going on at the same time outside Flor's house while the women meet inside, about fifty children in all.

RIGHT: Kids in USA: Our five Casa kids with their new family, the Sterlings; and our two Casa de Paz girls with their new family, the Guiers. All seven kids were adopted by parents from the same church in the United States.

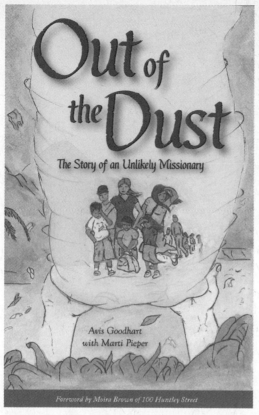

LEFT: Avis's son Mark Morgan's cover concept, depicting his mother's ministry in Peru.

BELOW: Sterling Family and president of Avila University on the Set of *The View*: (Left to Right) Scott Sterling, Sibila Sterling, Logan Sterling, Yhonny Sterling, Dr, Ronald Slepitza, Joel Sterling, Gerson Sterling, Betsi Sterling, Lauren Sterling with Laney Sterling on lap

Avis Goodhart, founder of Go Ye Ministries, is a missionary, Bible teacher, and conference speaker who has blessed audiences across North, South, and Central America. Although she holds a B.S.Ed. and M.Ed. from the University of Arkansas, her primary qualifications include the pain and obstacles she's encountered along the way. These provide both insight and passion for her work in bringing the lives of countless orphans, volunteers, and others out of the dust. Avis, a widow, has five children and twenty-two grandchildren.

Marti Pieper's prayer involvement moved her to assist Brent and Deanna Higgins in telling their son's story in *I Would Die for You*, which became a young adult bestseller. Marti, who has a B.S.Ed. from Ohio State University and an M.Div. from Southwestern Baptist Theological Seminary, has written multiple books and often teaches at writers' conferences.

American bush pilot Russell Stendal, on routine business, landed his plane in a remote Colombian village. Gunfire exploded throughout the town, and within minutes Russell's 142-day ordeal had begun. The Colombian cartel explained that this was a kidnapping for ransom and that he would be held until payment was made.

Held at gunpoint deep in the jungle and with little else to occupy his time, Russell asked for some paper and began to write. He told the story of his life and kept a record of his experience in the guerrilla camp. His "book" became a bridge to the men who held him hostage and now serves as the basis for this incredible true story of how God's love penetrated a physical and ideological jungle.

Purchase this book at http://amzn.to/Yv30YR